The Essential
Guide to...

OCD

HELP FOR FAMILIES AND FRIENDS

Dedication

To all the people living with OCD – I hope this book helps.

- First, it's not your fault!

- Secondly, take all the help the mental health people can give you – assuming it's a good team and they know about OCD.

- Thirdly, if you are a carer, find something outside the home that inspires you or is an affordable indulgence.

Mother of a daughter with OCD

The Essential Guide to...

OCD
HELP FOR FAMILIES AND FRIENDS

Helen Poskitt

LION

Published by Lion Books
an imprint of
Lion Hudson plc
Wilkinson House, Jordan Hill Road,
Oxford OX2 8DR, England
www.lionhudson.com/lion

ISBN 978 0 7459 5580 3
e-ISBN 978 0 7459 5715 9

First edition 2013

Acknowledgments
pp. 43–44: Extracts from *Obsessive Compulsive Disorder: The Facts* by Padmal
de Silva and Stanley Rackman copyright © de Silva/Rackman, 2009.
Reprinted by permission of Oxford University Press.

pp. 150–51: Extracts from JobAccess, an Australian government initiative:
http://jobaccess.gov.au. Reprinted by permission of JobAccess, Department
of Education, Employment and Workplace Relations.

A catalogue record for this book is available from the British Library

Printed and bound in the UK, January 2013, LH26

Contents

Acknowledgments

I am very grateful to all the selfless and cheerful OCD carers who made time to talk, bravely completed questionnaires, or welcomed me to their support groups. Without them, this book couldn't have been written. I also wish to thank the therapists who kindly contributed their time.

Most of the names of people mentioned in this book have been changed to preserve anonymity.

I

Introduction
· · · · · · · · · · · · · · · · · ·

This book is aimed at supporting relatives, friends and colleagues of people with Obsessive–Compulsive Disorder (OCD). It will enable carers to better understand how they can help individuals they know who have the condition. There is little doubt that a "hidden epidemic"[1] of OCD exists, but there is hope for both sufferers and carers.

Is mental illness the last taboo subject? Not any longer. Public figures such as MPs, celebrities and other role models are increasingly confessing to mental health problems such as OCD and depression. This, along with increased scientific research, is greatly reducing the old-fashioned stigma and secrecy associated with mental illness.

OCD is associated with a high IQ. It is thought in retrospect that Darwin, Beethoven, Dickens, Michelangelo, Churchill and Einstein, among other luminaries, suffered from the condition.

This condition is becoming more "visible" via popular television series, for example *Frasier, Monk* and *Friends*. OCD also features in films such as *As Good As it Gets, The Aviator* and *What's a Nice Girl Like You Doing in a Place Like This?*

WHAT IS OCD?

Robert Ackerman, an OCD expert, has memorably described OCD as a "cult of one". It can be difficult for people who don't experience OCD to understand why someone they know is behaving oddly. OCD has been classified as an anxiety disorder. Whatever we feel as onlookers, mocking or ignoring or trying to minimize the anxiety felt by an OCD sufferer will not make them feel better – just the opposite. They are experiencing a personal hell, however "normal" they may appear.

Families and/or carers can help people with OCD enormously, by learning about the condition and offering practical and emotional support. Helping does not mean colluding with the OCD sufferer's rituals and worries; but it does mean being kind, patient, and supportive.

How does OCD affect sufferers?

Many of us entertain satisfying scenarios of a terrible end for the motorist who has just almost involved us in an accident – but the thoughts (and motorist) quickly and harmlessly depart. The significance attached to such an idea by someone with OCD is where the problem lies. Despite their efforts to confront or ignore disturbing thoughts – of which there may be many – the ideas constantly reoccur. OCD sufferers therefore can experience fear, disgust and anxiety on a daily basis.

A person with OCD often carries out repetitive rituals to try to neutralize such upsetting thoughts. However, these compulsive rituals only provide short-term relief. They can easily escalate in frequency from a few times per day to hourly, as the action – for example, hand-washing – becomes less effective at combating the person's distress and self-doubt. The hand-washing ritual may be completely unconnected to worries about hygiene.

Compulsive rituals by OCD sufferers can include: *excessive* cleaning, washing, checking, repeated requests for reassurance, and hoarding. Practices also include: showing an aversion to/ preference for certain numbers; *repetitive* nervous actions such as switching lights on and off; checking that taps and cookers are turned off; entering and leaving rooms; checking the locks on doors. Note the italics above – there's nothing wrong with having a clean body, taking precautions against fire or flood, or checking that you've done your best to thwart burglars. The problem arises when the behaviour causes the individual with OCD to stop functioning adequately in daily life.

Few emotional disorders are as devastating as OCD. Patients often have difficulty with work, school, and in maintaining social and emotional relationships. When describing OCD, sufferers speak of being hyper-aware of everything happening around them. This naturally generates tension. Then factor in the brain sending false messages of danger to the person, in the form of obsessions, and stress predominates. Dr Jonathan Abramowitz, an OCD expert, says: "Sufferers undertake a measureless struggle... [against] recurrent thoughts, images, impulses and doubts that, although senseless on one hand, are perceived as danger signs on the other." When individuals can get a grip on their OCD – it is not easy – they recognize and re-label these false messages as "just an OCD thought", or powerless "ghosts and goblins".[2] They then understand that despite their nightmarish thoughts, nothing dangerous has happened after all.

In 1875, Legrand du Saulle referred to OCD as the *folie du doute* – "the doubting disease". Someone with OCD constantly doubts themselves, largely because their normal common sense is overwhelmed by sudden terrifying thoughts. It is very difficult for an OCD sufferer to access enough inner calmness to put these thoughts into perspective at the time. When an "OCD moment" hits, the person experiences the same panic as a parent would on seeing their child running into a busy road. It's easy, though, for an onlooker to underestimate the terror someone with OCD is experiencing, as sufferers understandably try to conceal it.

People with OCD may also "ruminate". This is when thoughts keep recurring for no apparent reason and revolve around a common theme. There is little difference between ruminations, obsessions and worries. They all trigger iterative (repetitive) thinking.

If we were to summarize in a simple format the thought processes of people suffering from OCD, it would run like this:

- *worries* typically focusing on daily concerns

- *obsessions* which may be more intrusive than worries

- obsessions then lead to *compulsions* and rituals (Turner *et al.*, 1992).

What links them all is *anxiety*. Altering the relationship between obsessions and compulsions centres on reducing this anxiety (Hodgson & Rachman, 1972; Rachman *et al.*, 1976).

OCD isn't made any easier to understand by the changeability of the symptoms. Many sufferers may only have one pattern or ritual of OCD behaviour throughout their lives; for instance, checking too often that the front door is locked. Others will have multiple obsessions and compulsions, such as checking, hoarding, washing, and contamination fears. Someone who has intrusive thoughts in adolescence may turn to washing excessively in early adulthood, and then become a "checker" in later life. On the other hand, many forms of repetitive behaviour may be mistakenly labelled as OCD. It's important to remember that to be defined as OCD, the pattern of behaviour must result in significant impairment, distress or anxiety, or become too time-consuming. It must take up more than an hour a day.

It is normal to have occasional thoughts about falling ill or concerning the safety of loved ones, without these being obsessions. Similarly, not all repetitive rituals are compulsions. Bedtime story-reading, religious practices or learning a new skill involve repeating an activity, but are a customary and often enjoyable part of daily life.

Someone you know with OCD might appear paranoid and their actions alienating, but it is worth emphasizing that people suffering from OCD are not mad; they usually recognize that their obsessions and compulsions are irrational and rarely act on them.

HOW COMMON IS OCD?

OCD isPa far more common than people realize. The condition has been estimated to affect 1 to 3 per cent of the population (National Institute for Clinical Excellence, 2005). Approximately 741,500 people in Britain are experiencing OCD at any given time, equating to twelve out of every 1,000 citizens. Less than a quarter of these cases could be classified as "mild", with the rest being "severe". It has been suggested that 2 to 3 per cent of people visiting their doctor will be doing so concerning OCD – it is diagnosed almost as often as asthma in the UK. OCD is also very egalitarian. It affects people regardless of their race, religion, sex or socio-economic group. It is the fourth most common mental disorder in many Western countries. It's not just a Western disorder, though: according to a study in 2008,[3] Japanese OCD patients show similar symptoms to those in the West. The condition transcends geography and culture.

In the USA, it is estimated that about 1 in 100 adults – or between 2 and 3 million adults – currently have OCD. This is a similar figure to that of the population of Houston, Texas. There are also at least 1 in 200 – or 500,000 – children and teenagers with OCD (statistically the same as youngsters who suffer from diabetes).

The ratio of female to male OCD sufferers is pretty equal in the adolescent population. It is estimated to be 1.5:1.0 in the community as a whole. However, men predominate in surveys of OCD referrals – perhaps reflecting more acute illness in males.

DIAGNOSIS AND MISDIAGNOSIS

Many people believe that the sooner OCD is identified and treated, the better the chance of recovery. The organization OCD-UK advises, for example, that early intervention is vital. It's therefore important to have a correct diagnosis. Even if the patient has had OCD for a long time, there is still a chance of successfully treating the illness. (The average time between onset of OCD and diagnosis is sixteen years.) An accurate diagnosis will greatly help in the process of improving the quality of life for both sufferer and carer.

Normally following a visit to the GP, formal diagnosis may then be performed by a psychologist, psychiatrist, clinical social worker or other licensed mental health professional. To be diagnosed with OCD, a person must have obsessions, compulsions, or both, according to the Diagnostic and Statistical Manual of Mental Disorders (DSM).

OCD is diagnosed on the basis of a psychiatric examination, a history of the patient's symptoms and complaints and the degree to which the symptoms interfere with daily functioning. Based on the nature, length and frequency of the symptoms presented, the doctor will differentiate OCD from other diseases with similar symptoms. These include phobias, schizophrenia, panic disorder and generalized anxiety disorder. A physical examination may also be ordered, to rule out other causes of the symptoms. As yet, there is no blood test available with which to reliably diagnose the condition.

There are several tools that mental health professionals use to aid a diagnosis of OCD. The Yale-Brown Obsessive–Compulsive Scale (YBOCS) is a questionnaire used to help target obsessive–compulsive symptoms and to assess their severity. It's also used to monitor and assess clinical response to treatment.

Other means of assessment include the:

- Compulsive Activity Checklist (CAC)

- Leyton Obsessional Inventory (LOI)

- Maudsley Obsessive Compulsive Inventory (MOCI)

- Padua Inventory (PI)

- NIMH Global Obsessive–Compulsive Scale (NIMH Global OC).

Despite this, it's not surprising that there's a risk of occasionally misdiagnosing OCD. Abramowitz believes that the psychopathology is among the most complicated of the emotional disorders. The wide array and intricate associations between behavioural and mental symptoms can puzzle even the most experienced clinicians.

There is a clear relationship between OCD and depression: they are commonly linked. Many people with OCD are likely to have a history of bouts of depression, during which the symptoms of the condition tend to worsen. Some people develop obsessions when they become depressed; these obsessions are usually secondary to the depression and depart when the misery lifts. Some patients become depressed following the onset of OCD.[4]

One therapist recommends that an OCD sufferer with depression should visit a GP or psychiatrist for consideration of anti-depressant treatment. This should include a full explanation of side-effects and long-term outcome, such as the possibility that OCD will recur when the client discontinues anti-depressants.

Major features of depression are:

- seriously depressed mood

- loss of interest or pleasure in usual activities

- disturbance of appetite and sleep

- severe slowing or agitation
- feelings of worthlessness or extreme guilt
- extensive pessimism and suicidal ideas.

On the diagnosis front, OCD is often confused with a separate condition: obsessive–compulsive personality disorder (OCPD). The difference between these is that when someone has OCD, it goes against the sufferer's view of themselves. This can cause them to feel very upset. OCPD, on the other hand, is shown by the patient's acceptance that the characteristics of this illness are consistent with their own self-image. OCD sufferers are anxiety-ridden and often aware that their behaviour is irrational. People with OCPD, though, often derive pleasure from their obsessions or compulsions. They usually believe their actions are rational.

In 1998,[5] it was found that only 6 to 25 per cent of people with OCD have full-blown OCPD. When a person with OCD also has OCPD, characteristics such as rigidity, perfectionism and the need for control can make the OCD behaviour more difficult to alter. This is mainly due to the OCPD person's reluctance to accept guidance from without, as this implies they are less than "perfect". When they finally do accept that they have a need, though, there is opportunity for change.

Another thing that might complicate diagnosis is when someone has acute OCD and also holds an unshakeable belief stemming from the illness. This can make the condition difficult to differentiate from psychosis. OCD is different from gambling, addiction and overeating disorders. People who have these usually gain at least some joy from their activity. Individuals with OCD do not want to perform their compulsive tasks and don't experience any pleasure while doing them.

Many years ago, some clinicians believed OCD and schizophrenia to be closely related. This has now been discredited.[6] The chances of an OCD patient becoming schizophrenic are no higher than for any other person. Nevertheless, people with OCD are sometimes misdiagnosed as schizophrenic. This is largely due to the superficial similarity between obsessions and the delusions that schizophrenics commonly hold. In the early stages of schizophrenia, obsessions and compulsions may occasionally appear, but are short-lived. Schizophrenics' unwanted thoughts are usually ones that the patient believes to have been placed in their minds by external forces (human or otherwise). This feature makes these very different from OCD obsessions, which the patient recognizes as their own.

What therapists say

OCD is only difficult to diagnose initially if there is a reluctance to talk about it by the client.
Barbara Hodges

OCD isn't difficult to diagnose – often people have already decided they have it and tell you what they think you need to hear. While clients don't like the habits and rituals they perform, they like the label of OCD. It provides a rational reason regarding their problems. Of course, sometimes they are wrong!

OCD sits so easily with a person who may have a tendency to be overly tidy, studies extensively, etc. Reading about obsessiveness on the Internet means they can swiftly tick many boxes. The person then assumes they have OCD, when in fact they are merely a bit stressed, or only have borderline OCD.
Irene Tubbs

It's not been difficult to diagnose people, as my clients have come to me saying they would like treatment for OCD. They were all GP-referred, directly or indirectly. Strangely, I've found my clients don't trawl the Internet or check out other sources of information about OCD. Most patients are surprised that others suffer in the same way as they do.

Most of the people I've met with OCD are desperate to be treated. They believe the condition is taking many aspects of their life away, so that they no longer enjoy partaking in activities that others take for granted.
Dawn Cook

WHAT TRIGGERS OCD?

OCD can strike out of the blue, at any age. Something we might consider trivial, such as a comment by a family member, has been known to trigger the onset of OCD. At other times, a traumatic incident is responsible. A major crisis, such as bereavement, leaving home, divorce, or the discovery of health problems, can also trigger it. Other events, even supposedly joyful ones such as marriage, may do the same.

....

Interview: Emma

I met an ex-colleague, Emma, for a sandwich lunch. She looked strained.

Helen, since we got married three months ago, Tony's been acting really strangely. When he washes his hands, he soaps them for ages and then I hear the water running and he's doing it again, twenty minutes later. On our honeymoon, I joked about it, but I'm finding it really difficult now, and his poor hands are all red and sore. I wouldn't be so bothered if it was just that; it is huge, getting married. I thought it might just be a temporary nervous thing he's going through.

What else is Tony doing?

He keeps checking the cooker's off and the taps are off. Oh, and a new one, since yesterday – whether he's locked the garage door properly. It takes him ages to leave for work in the morning. We're not talking just the once; he checks things over and over again.

I know something about this: my uncle used to do similar things.

On Monday, Tony went back to the kitchen to check the cooker eight times, and the last time I heard him talking to himself. It was scary. This is all since we got married; he never did it before.

Well, how much time did you spend together before you got married?

The odd night during the week and most weekends, but he was away for that month on business in Germany... I suppose not that much. We were on Skype and email a lot, though.

So perhaps Tony had these worries then, but managed to hide them. People with OCD are often secretive: they feel ashamed of their thoughts. How are you managing? Have you talked to Tony?

Yes, and I've tried to reassure him about other things he's worried about. They sound silly, to be honest – even weird. All about spreading disease and making other people ill. But sometimes I feel as though I'm talking to myself. It's as though Tony doesn't believe me. He just asks me to repeat myself. It's really hurtful. I feel disloyal talking about him like this. I'm worried he'll lose his job. He's getting later and later leaving home in the morning. I have to promise I'll do the checking for him, though he still does it a bit before he goes. Do you think he's going mad?

No. It sounds like OCD.

But we're supposed to be happy. Tony sounded so keen on getting married.

Perhaps he feels it's down to him to make sure it works, and you don't regret getting together with him. People with OCD feel hugely responsible for everything.

Did you say your uncle had it?

Yes, Uncle Bill had OCD. He did similar things to Tony, but he had other hang-ups as well. There was a rug in the hall at home. Uncle Bill lived down the road, and when he came round he had to step on and off this rug in a particular way. I think it was to do with touching it a certain number of times or something… It got quite embarrassing. I think we laughed at him. But that was a long time ago, and nowadays we know a lot more about OCD.

I don't know anyone else who's got it.

I bet you do – they just hide it. A lot of people have it, mildly. It's as common as diabetes. It's only a problem when it stops you functioning.

But Tony never showed it before we got married. It must be my fault.

Of course it's not – people can be affected by OCD at any time. I think it might be triggered by stress and, as you said, marriage is a big event.

The trouble is, Tony doesn't talk to me about normal things any more. He's either silent or irritable, or worrying about something.

My uncle explained it to me once. He said that people with OCD have upsetting and intrusive thoughts that make them feel really anxious.

But virtually everyone has inappropriate thoughts…

This is different, Emma. Normally people can forget bad thoughts quickly. If you've got OCD, you can't get the ideas out of your head. They just go round and round. The person often feels really guilty. Do you want to do a quick exercise? Close your eyes and don't think about yellow flamingos for the next minute. I'll time you…Time's up! So how did you do?

I kept seeing beautiful bouncing flamingos! I couldn't help it.

Now imagine that you thinking about those exotic creatures will cause harm to a woman standing near you. Replace the thought of those flamingos with a horrific vision of murdering this poor woman. The more you try to avoid thinking about it, the more insistent the idea becomes.

You're not saying Tony's going to kill people?

No. It's very rare for people with OCD to do whatever they're obsessing about. Poor old Tony's probably horrified today by thoughts of burning down your flat by leaving the cooker on. He's also possibly convinced he's going mad. But he's not. Do you remember Alex from work last year? I caught him tapping the paper in the photocopier, again and again, for no reason. I pretended not to notice, but I think it was OCD. He looked really worried when he thought I'd seen him. Loads of people have it. In fact, if you look at Tony's behaviour positively, he's just über-concerned for your safety.

So what's all this with rattling the garage door lock umpteen times?

As I understand it, repetitive rituals help people with OCD to neutralize the awful thoughts. Trouble is, it only provides short-term relief, so they carry out the actions more and more often, and that becomes another difficulty.

Is there a cure?

Not as such. But something called CBT comes highly recommended. There's medication, too.

What's CBT?

Cognitive Behavioural Therapy. It's a talking remedy. People see a therapist who helps them to challenge the frightening thoughts and the rituals. It's like re-educating the mind – it has a high success rate.

....

OCD triggered by giving birth

If you have a close relative who is pregnant, whether they currently have OCD or not, it is worth being aware that the stress of giving birth can trigger OCD. The arrival of a new baby presents unfamiliar challenges and this can prove overwhelming for some women. The time period soon after giving birth (called the "postpartum" period) may be particularly hard for women who do not have adequate coping strategies or support in place to help them.[7] If the mother already has OCD, she can experience worsening symptoms. Male partners are not exempt and may also develop OCD soon after the new baby arrives. Experts are unsure of the exact figures for Postpartum OCD (PPOCD), but estimate it affects 2 to 3 per cent of new mothers. It usually occurs around three and a half weeks after the birth. Women with PPOCD have reported experiencing both obsessions and compulsions; the obsessive thoughts were aggressive and involved their babies. None of them acted on their obsessions to harm their children, but five women taking part in a study reported dysfunctional mother–child behaviour.

It's thought that the main difference between PPOCD and the OCD affecting the general population is that new mothers who develop it tend to focus their obsessive thoughts on their baby. Women with PPOCD are acutely aware that their feelings are abnormal. Some mothers with the disorder are reluctant to seek help, though, fearing that they will be treated with disdain. It is important that women affected by PPOCD seek professional help. Left untreated, it can impede a woman's ability to cope, as well as interfere in her relationship with her child, partner, family and friends.

Signs of PPOCD include:[8]

- intrusive, recurrent and obsessive thoughts – usually involving the baby

- avoidance behaviour – possibly of the baby, but generally of anything that will cause fear

- anxiety and/or depression

- fear

- establishing rituals, which include repetitive behaviour, such as touching every door knob they pass; obsessive cleaning and/or washing; hoarding – this is done to combat fear of losing objects.

Women with Postpartum OCD also suffer more obsessions about contaminating their infant than mothers who don't have this condition.

Mothers affected by PPOCD usually experience obsessive thoughts about their baby coming to harm. This can result in repetitive behaviour, such as repeatedly sterilizing the baby's bottle for fear of contamination, or checking on the child an excessive number of times. Some women may also fear hurting their child in some way, such as drowning the baby during bath-time. While these anxieties can be particularly disturbing, very few mothers with this disorder are likely to cause themselves or their child any harm.

Although any woman has the potential to develop PPOCD, mothers who have a personal or family history of OCD are at increased risk of developing it. Women who develop an obsessive–compulsive disorder during pregnancy are more than twice as likely to have PPOCD. In women who have pre-existing OCD, there is evidence that miscarriage can also act as a trigger for the condition.

In the following interview, a child's OCD was triggered by domestic violence towards her mother, and the ensuing divorce.

....

Interview: Suzanne, Amanda's mother

The past few years have been very stressful. We've lived in many locations, most of which were less than ideal. This follows on from my divorce. I was in a marriage that involved domestic violence. My child is with my ex part of the time, and life there has been unstable as well.

When did you first think Amanda might have OCD?

Second grade was when I really noticed OCD symptoms. Prior to that, Amanda had stomach aches, nightmares and a general heightened anxiety. She had several behaviours that were related to stress.

How did you know it was OCD?

Well, at first I didn't. I began to observe that she washed her hands frequently. When I first noticed that, I started to mentally track and realized that she washed her hands upwards of forty times a day. In fact she reached a point of fifty times or more.

That must have been really hard to deal with.

At the time, I told myself that this was a reaction to her school's obsession with hand-washing. Swine flu had hit the state. Amanda had sat through an assembly, had nurses come in and speak to her class, and was asked to use the instant hand sanitizer before and after every activity. The school frightened the children with germs and what they could do if not washed away. Many kids were walking around with red, sore hands.

What happened then?

I noticed the "touching". If Amanda bumped the wall with her left hand, she turned and bumped it with her right. If she brushed against a counter with her stomach, she turned and touched her back to the same counter. When I asked her why, she said she had to – "I have to be fair." I didn't react with alarm to this. So much in her life had been "not fair" that I figured this might be a kid way of processing and dealing with things. We were in a safe place by then; I thought maybe Amanda now felt relaxed enough to start healing from the past few years.

Soon though, I noticed my daughter counting steps. Soon afterwards she wasn't able to touch a fork if someone else had touched it first, or a cup. Then she wasn't able to handle being touched. If someone accidentally brushed against her arm or hand, she freaked. She was counting words; they had to be even numbered like her steps. She refused to touch door knobs and many other things. I learned Amanda was not using the bathroom at school because she would not touch the door.

Did the school provide any help?

Her teacher called me in for a meeting. It was to her I first used the expression "OCD", as in: "Do you think that might be what we are looking at?"

Does Amanda carry out any other rituals?

Yes, she touches the car when we load up in a way that makes sense to her and says she must do it to be safe. She doesn't know what she will be safe from, just that she is in danger if she doesn't do things in a certain way. She dresses in a certain way, too. She does not want to do any of this; she feels she has to.

Is she also coping with obsessive thoughts and worries, without performing any rituals?

She is. If she hears a police or ambulance siren, she assumes the world is ending. She worries if adults are late for work or not, if the other kids in her class are doing their homework, if homeless dogs are hungry, if I am going to die... On and on.

It must help her a lot, being able to talk to you. Does she have any other coping mechanisms?

Amanda has learned to call OCD a monster. She sees it as a larger than life thing which overpowers her every day. She thinks she is a freak, because people look at her – usually when she is licking her clothing. It makes her mad at herself; my child hates herself. She said once, "If this is how it is always going to be, I don't want to live." So she is not coping.

What do you find helps you to get through this?

I talk with people who understand OCD and who can give me pointers on how best to talk with Amanda and guide her through this process. I read books to better educate myself. I attempt to model "calm". Unfortunately, my ex-husband has a voice in our child receiving professional help. He stands in opposition. He feels our daughter needs to "Knock it off" and "Even if it is real, your mother caused it". He denies that any of these behaviours are seen at their house; this breaks my daughter's heart.

Has your relationship with your daughter altered since the onset of the illness?

In some ways... I can't fight this fight for her. I can't take on this monster, but I can cheer her on as she does. She knows she can admit her fears, her "weaknesses", to me. She knows she doesn't have to pretend to be tough. All of that is huge.

How have Amanda's other relatives and friends reacted?

Many read up on OCD so they can talk with me about it.

And school staff?

The teachers care and they try, so overall they've been very supportive. Amanda's third-grade teacher, though, was overwhelmed with too many kids, many of them with big issues. She noticed my child was "fidgety", but nothing beyond that. She had no idea what Amanda was going through each day – what it took for her to pick up a pencil she knew had been touched by someone else, or how much energy went into tracking the progress, emotions and happiness of all the kids in the class. Just watching what they all touched, so she knew what she could/could not handle was a full-time job for my daughter. This teacher got kind of hard on Amanda for a "lack of effort" towards the end of the year. She assumed she was being lazy. Amanda had to erase almost everything she wrote and write it again to "get it right". She had to read each paragraph twice (even numbers). She had to touch each part of the pencil on every spot (to be fair) and it is challenging to have good penmanship when you are holding the very end of a pencil.

So, while I don't like making excuses for my child, I do wish the teacher had understood better. She gave her a grade 3 instead of a 4 on her report card, and Amanda was devastated. The mark indicated a lack of effort. I was unable to talk with the teacher, by the way, because of the fallout from my ex if he were to hear of it. His desire for power and control hasn't ended and he still plays games.

Does Amanda experience any bullying or discrimination due to her OCD?

Kids ask her why she does this or that. She tells them, "It's just what I do", but that works less well with the passing years.

Has anything else changed due to the OCD – the interior of your home, or holidays you might take?

No. At first I did make an effort to accommodate Amanda's growing fears of germs and such, but I learned to not do that. My family wanted to show support by doing this as well, but have since learned to check that impulse.

Did you find it difficult getting information about OCD?

Information about OCD? No. Information about how best to support me and my child? Yes.

Was the medical profession helpful?

I took Amanda to a counsellor, who proved to be pretty unhelpful. She lacked understanding about domestic violence, so lacked knowledge on how to deal with my ex.

How about a local support group?

No. Such groups, in my experience, focus on what's wrong with the kid, instead of what's right.

What do you wish someone had told you early on, that might have made things easier for you?

How to support my child and talk with her about the OCD, without accommodating it.

Do you find things like changes in diet are useful to help combat OCD? For you too, in terms of energy?

Amanda struggles more with too much TV, lack of sleep, and too many processed foods. She does better with healthy food, a lot of nature time – being outdoors is fun – and only watching a bit of TV. The obvious stuff.

Does exercise help?

I have her in Aikido, and a mentoring/running programme.

Exercise is very helpful for her. Me, too!

Would you give me one piece of advice to pass on to someone who has just discovered that someone close to them has OCD?

Remember, you just noticed, but they have been dealing with OCD for a time now. So, this is not a crisis. Slow down, educate yourself. Learn how to avoid "feeding" this OCD monster.

....

Interview: Joyce, Ben's mother

Exam stress has been known to trigger OCD, as in the following case:

Ben's OCD was brought on by exam stress; he's had it since he sat his A-levels when he was eighteen. He was very bad with it again during his degree Finals. I guessed my son had OCD when he kept washing his hands. The doctor confirmed it and tried to help, but he wasn't very knowledgeable. I've found that since with other doctors.

Ben still washes his hands too often and he also keeps checking the soles of his shoes. He worries obsessively about whether he's caused an accident when he's out driving. He ends up redoing car journeys. I thought the OCD might improve when Ben bought his new flat, but it's worse now. He keeps it obsessively clean; going to see him isn't very relaxing. I try to stay supportive and not get angry with him. My husband (now deceased) used to belittle my son concerning his illness; so did my in-laws sometimes.

My relationship with Ben has changed. My son will now talk to me about his illness, and actually attended the OCD Action Conference. He also accepts that if he's staying or living back at home with me, he cannot control dirt there. I have four cats! Ben won't use towels, though, so I constantly replenish tissues.

I learned quite a lot about OCD from books, OCD Action and No Panic – there aren't any local support groups. Ben tried three different anti-depressants, but took himself off them due to side-effects such as constipation. He also said they made him feel like a zombie.

....

PUBLIC AWARENESS

What therapists say

Public knowledge has got much better in the last decade (probably because of the Internet and other media) but is still insufficient. There needs to be more information out there about OCD.
Simon Morton

If you look at statistics, awareness of OCD has improved. This has resulted in more people willing to openly discuss an experience that they previously thought of as weird. This doesn't mean that there's a rise in OCD across the population – just that people are "coming out of the closet".
Megan Karnes

Unfortunately there isn't enough public knowledge or understanding about OCD. I don't think for example that educational establishments for those under eighteen will necessarily have much understanding of students with OCD.
Angela Bennett

People without OCD may occasionally be frightened by OCD behaviour; daily life can be scary for clients too. They often struggle with tasks and events the rest of us take for granted.
Angela Bennett

*I believe that mental health is stigmatized and
not given the appropriate support, because people
are frightened. Things might improve if we all
understood conditions such as psychosis, bipolar
disorder and depression.*
Megan Karnes

Therapists do not agree on whether or not there will be a cure
for OCD within the next twenty years.

2

OCD Obsessions

. . . .

Obsessions are usually much more intrusive than typical worries, and may not always relate to daily concerns. They will often result in rituals being performed to ease the anxiety. (Rituals are explained further in Chapter 3.)

Common obsessions of OCD sufferers revolve around:

- contamination
- causing harm to others or self
- symmetry
- "safe" numbers and "good" words
- scrupulosity/religiosity
- sexual themes
- rumination.

CONTAMINATION

This obsession manifests itself in an exaggerated fear of dirt, germs or illness. Those with OCD may also experience "mental contamination", which affects the thoughts, perhaps triggered by verbal abuse or insults. The person feels dirty even though they haven't been in physical contact with an object.

CAUSING HARM TO OTHERS OR SELF

People with OCD feel hyper-responsible for others, to the point that they mentally anticipate potential disaster constantly. They are very frightened of causing harm to anyone else, and this may also extend to fears about their own health. The latter is manifested by a dread of illness and terror of dying early.

Hit 'n' Run OCD

This is associated with a fear of harming others too. Many adults with OCD find driving difficult to cope with, because it is accompanied by an obsessive terror of causing an accident. Although they sound the least likely motorists to have an accident, a person with OCD holding a UK driving licence needs to tell the licensing authorities about their OCD if it affects their ability to drive safely.

Driving involves being in charge of a machine which can cause injury and death to others, so it fits perfectly with hyper-responsibility anxieties. Progress with overcoming driving fears needs acceptance of the risks inherent in living life fully. Someone with OCD can feel so scared that they don't feel fully in charge of their own life. Experiencing life to the full can be hijacked by an OCD sufferer's need to try to control events over which people as a whole have very little control.

As with scrupulosity (being careful to behave morally) and checking patterns of behaviour, the person with hit 'n' run OCD believes that unless they are constantly on guard, disaster will strike. When driving, they are convinced they will run over a person or an animal, causing injury or death. Guilt and retribution will ensue. The OCD motorist may not see any animals or people on the roads along which they drive on a particular journey. This won't necessarily stop them feeling it is imperative to immediately repeat the trip, to check they haven't caused any harm. The driver may also exhaustively examine their vehicle for damage or other evidence that they have hit a person or animal, when they reach their destination.

SYMMETRY

This is where people with OCD need their possessions, or aspects of their surroundings, arranged symmetrically. Books might be placed exactly on top of each other and at an exact right angle to the edge of a table; pens and pencils could be lined up with geometric precision, etc. An OCD sufferer might also move in symmetrical ways.

"SAFE" NUMBERS AND "GOOD" WORDS

OCD sufferers often use numbers for reassurance – constantly counting things, such as steps, so as to emerge at a "right" or "safe" number. The person might also "cancel out/undo" a "bad" word with a "good" one.

SCRUPULOSITY/RELIGIOSITY

This aspect of OCD is characterized by pathological guilt about moral or religious issues. Someone with scrupulosity OCD is very concerned to behave morally. They will probably be preoccupied with religious matters, such as the afterlife, death or morality. (This is not to be confused with normal religious belief, which is not accompanied by the same obsessions.) People with this form of OCD sometimes pray a lot. Although scrupulosity is often categorized as OCD, it would seem to be more fitted to OCPD. The term is derived from the Latin *scrupulum*, "a sharp stone", implying a stabbing pain on the conscience – an apt description of the anguish it can cause sufferers.

SEXUAL THEMES

Imagine you are a young heterosexual man seated on a London underground train, and an elderly man is sitting opposite you in the narrow carriage. A random thought of violently sexually molesting this man cuts across your mind. Frightened and disgusted, you try to ignore it, but the scenario sticks, becoming more lurid by the second. You glance quickly across at the passenger to ensure you haven't said or done anything to him. He looks fine. It makes no difference to the distressing thoughts; they don't go away. It feels increasingly as though you have actually assaulted this man. You look at him again to check his well-being; this time he stares back at you, perplexed.

Embarrassed, you stand up with other passengers to disembark at a station, making exaggerated efforts not to touch the man in the confined space. Unfortunately a child is also trying to get off the train: more horrible and violent thoughts crowd into your mind. You try to avoid being anywhere near the child. Once on the platform, you stop – much to the irritation of the crowds trying to get past – and watch the train leave. You are straining to see if the elderly man is unscathed in his carriage, while simultaneously trying to locate the child among the crowd of departing people to ensure she too hasn't been molested by you. Somewhere in the panic, you know you haven't touched these people – but the anxiety is a mental holocaust. The following month, such thoughts might change to fears about incest, or of harming your baby niece.

These unwanted sexual obsessive thoughts and resisted impulses greatly distress the OCD sufferer. They can also deeply and adversely affect relationships. You may have been on the receiving end of a confusing change of behaviour from someone you love; perhaps they begin making excuses not to see you. A formerly loving grandmother with OCD begins avoiding her young grandchildren. An OCD sufferer may stop babysitting, or start to avoid friends and relatives with children. Parents become literally unable to touch their children, due to the

OCD fear of molesting or harming them. Mothers who suffer OCD onset after giving birth find daily life hellish.

Other OCD sexual obsessions can include fears regarding a person's own sexuality. A person with OCD can begin questioning their sexual orientation – a normal phase for many people, but they feel tormented by the subject.

Interview: Mary

My son's obsessions centred mainly round sexual topics. For a time, he obsessed over harming others in a sexual way – molesting people – and spreading semen. Past rituals have included hand-washing, seeking reassurance, him yelling out "bad thought", pulling at his clothes and walking only on certain areas of the floor.

Glenn's eighteen now and is currently free of OCD, but it started when he was very young. It then hit him with a vengeance when he reached fourteen years old. From the age of five, Glenn did have episodes – they lasted from a few weeks to several months – when his OCD would flare up, but these always faded away. I knew we were dealing with OCD because I am a paediatrician and was able to make the diagnosis when my son's symptoms became severe, more focused. Before then, I just assumed he was an anxious child.

Glenn is now at college and taking honours courses; his grades are good; he has friends. When things were bad, I coped by reading, reading, and reading about OCD. To help him, I studied as much as I could about the condition, using as many different sources as possible. I didn't have any problems finding information: I raided libraries, the Internet, and ordered books. To me, knowledge was the key. The more I understood, the more I felt we could deal with the illness.

With hindsight, I wish someone had said early on: "Don't wait it out. Engage with the OCD symptoms the minute you see them. Don't let the obsessions take hold!" The longer the symptoms are allowed to fester, the longer it takes and the harder it is to recover from OCD. My relationship with my son has altered, of course. If you're close to someone who has OCD, I can't imagine your relationship not being affected by it. At the beginning of Glenn's illness, our relationship was definitely more intense because of his many symptoms. But overall we remain very close.

For me to deal with my son's illness I had to quit working and focus on helping him through life. The most difficult change was to the relationship with my husband. He didn't understand and couldn't accept that our son had problems that needed serious interventions. His approach was simply to yell louder, or to instil more discipline. We did not confide in other members of the family for a long time, because we knew they wouldn't be able to help us, or understand. Glenn and I eventually told them, but they never asked many questions, read any books on OCD or even acknowledged the pain we'd been through until Glenn wrote a book on his experience. After reading his book, family members did seem to understand a little more.

Other people haven't been very supportive. They simply don't understand OCD and we've given up trying to tell them. Our doctor wasn't helpful. In fact very little help was given by any of Glenn's mental health professionals. From my experience, I would say to be very careful about choosing therapists and physicians: too many of them think they know how to treat OCD, but don't. I think there's a large need for OCD support groups. There aren't any close by, so I'm considering setting one up.

Luckily Glenn hasn't been bullied or discriminated against. He's very good at hiding his symptoms when he has OCD, like lots of people with the condition. He knew if anyone around him, other than family, knew about his OCD, he would probably experience problems. We didn't feel comfortable telling anyone at Glenn's school about his disorder, as we didn't feel they had an understanding of the condition.

We experimented with changing his diet, but it made no difference. Glenn and I exercise often though; we both think it helps quell the anxiety.

Obsessive thinking about sex is not uncommon, particularly in young adults, but it can distress and dominate an OCD sufferer's thoughts. They might do some disturbing writing or doodling of a sexual nature.

....

RUMINATION

A person with OCD might also excessively ruminate. This is also known as Pure Obsessional OCD. Their thoughts keep recurring for no apparent reason and revolve around a common theme. Because these reflections tend to be about unsuccessfully reaching a desired goal, the sufferer feels distressed.

Some ruminative thought is perfectly normal, perhaps as a response to stress, or as a means of achieving something. However, if the thought process fails to reach natural closure, there can be problems. People with OCD cannot adapt their thoughts properly and so continue to unprofitably and unhappily brood.

An individual with this aspect of OCD will not usually carry out any physical compulsive rituals, so excessive rumination can be harder to detect. Ritualizing and neutralizing activities do take place, but are almost all in the form of thought.

Ironically, even though the child or adult with "Pure-O" is concentrating so hard inwardly, they may be accused of lacking concentration at school or in the workplace. This is because they might not be engaging with the activity they are supposed to be doing.

Obsessions and rumination are difficult to tell apart, as they need not centre round daily matters and both cause intrusive thoughts.

A therapist says

> *When a client is ruminating, they can see themselves*
> *as not performing a ritual, and it's harder to have*
> *them challenge the OCD thought patterns.*
> **Megan Karnes**

ARE OCD SUFFERERS DISABLED?

This appears to be a grey area: people with OCD are not officially disabled in the UK. However, OCD can be classed as a disability (at the point of diagnosis) under the Equality Act 2010. The Act states that employers are not allowed to discriminate against disabled people. Some people with OCD apply for Disability Living Allowance (DLA).

What therapists say

> *It's difficult to generalize about whether people with*
> *severe OCD are disabled.*
> **Kate Rumble**

> *Mental ill-health is a recognized disorder; I would*
> *say that people with OCD are disabled.*
> **Megan Karnes**

> *People with severe OCD are not officially disabled.*
> *(There is insufficient time devoted to OCD on many*
> *training courses; hence it is seen as a difficult and*
> *complex condition.)*
> **Catherine Philips**

> *I believe people who have severe OCD are effectively*
> *disabled.*
> **Dawn Cook**

3

Compulsions and Rituals

. . . .

OCD obsessions often lead to compulsions. A person with OCD will experience an almost overwhelming compulsion to perform certain patterns of behaviour, or rituals. This is done to try to stop their anxiety. These rituals have sometimes been compared to superstitious behaviour; this view can help people without OCD to understand the condition better.

Rituals include *excessive*:

- washing and cleaning

- checking

- symmetry

- counting; for example, number of steps

- repeating/redoing tasks unnecessarily

- praying

- hoarding.

FEAR OF CONTAMINATION

Television advertisements selling anti-bacterial household products encourage the public to view the idea of germs with exaggerated fear and disgust. But this is how OCD sufferers have always felt. OCD sufferers have always obsessed fearfully about the risk of "contamination". Washing or cleaning rituals are often performed many times by a person with OCD, until they "feel" that they or their surroundings are clean. This contrasts with the behaviour of someone without OCD, who will carry out an action only once, or until they "see" that cleanliness has been achieved. Too much washing or cleaning will often damage the skin, especially on the hands. Then there is the cost of frequently purchased cleaning products. Replacing items that have become damaged due to excessive use of liquid may also prove expensive.

The person with OCD can be affected by "mental contamination" as well. The feelings of mental contamination share several qualities with "contact contamination", but have some distinctive features. One is that the source of mental contamination is almost always human. Feelings of mental contamination may be evoked when a person feels badly treated, physically or mentally, through critical or verbally abusive remarks. It is almost as if they are made to feel like dirt, which creates a feeling of internal uncleanness. The person with OCD will engage in repetitive and compulsive attempts to wash away the dirt – similar to the response to "traditional" OCD contamination anxieties.

The OCD thought process of someone with contamination fears could well run like this. They contract athlete's foot and are then told by a friend that this germ can cause sexually transmitted infections (STIs). The young man with OCD now washes his hands diligently every time he thinks he's put them anywhere near his feet. Even if he hasn't touched them, he's so scared that he quickly doubts his own judgment. Soon, he becomes paranoid about sleeping with his partner. This is in case he transmits the athlete's foot fungus to anywhere on his partner's body, either from his own hands or feet, or via other parts of his body that he's inadvertently touched and not washed since touching his feet.

By this time, the OCD sufferer might also be silently agonizing as to whether the germs can be transmitted via his clothing. He doesn't know, as he can't see germs, but would rather err on the side of caution. By now, he is in a permanent state of fear near other people, particularly his partner, in case they have an STI from his athlete's foot somewhere on their body and clothing. This infection having taken hold might get worse, and – as if that's not anxiety enough – what if his partner is being unfaithful? They'll have passed the germs on to someone else! The world, already frightening and overwhelming, begins to implode for the person with OCD. Their partner, on the other hand, is feeling upset and wondering what they've done wrong. All their loving overtures are being spurned. The relationship will probably break down due to miscommunication: STIs won't even enter the equation.

Another self-sabotaging anxiety for someone with OCD can be of acting as the "carrier" of a disease, without displaying any symptoms themselves.

A case illustration from *Obsessive Compulsive Disorder: The Facts* describes a young woman's contamination anxieties:

> … *Her main concern was about excrement, both human and animal. She would wash extensively after returning from a walk even if she did not actually see, let alone step on, dirt. This was because she felt that dog dirt is spread all over the roads and pavements by rain and wind. She would leave her shoes at the door and change into a different pair before entering the house. She totally avoided public toilets. As the problem got worse, she began to avoid going anywhere near manholes as they indicated the presence of sewers with human excreta underneath … By the time she came for help, she had almost wholly stopped going out, had left her job as a result*

> *and had begun to spend most of her time in bed. She*
> *had also begun to demand that her parents, with*
> *whom she lived, stop going out, as they would bring*
> *dirt into the house when they returned, and to insist*
> *that they left their shoes outside and washed their*
> *hands and feet when they returned from an outing.*[1]

We can see the impact here not only on the OCD sufferer's life, but on those close to her. If someone spends a lot of time cleaning and obsessing about perceived hazards, they have less time or inclination to socialize.

If the disorder is acute, as above, people with OCD will become restricted in their activities. They may avoid places – for instance, crowded shops or public loos – where they've experienced contamination fears before. They might stop shaking hands when introduced to people, due to their fear of germs. A person with OCD may also refuse to invite visitors to their home, in case they bring in germs or dust.

....

Interview: Jeremy

You mentioned that your wife cleans exhaustively if you're expecting visitors to your home. Even if it's family or friends?

That's right. When we met, in our twenties, her flat was always shiny and clean. I didn't think anything of it; it was just a nice place to stay. I was sharing a house with mates at the time – all men. I found it endearing, my girlfriend being particular. I used to joke, but I was quite proud of it.

Did you have a more relaxed home set-up when you were growing up?

Yes. Not dirty really, but relaxed – more normal. My mum's quite casual. There were three of us children and we always had pets, and friends coming round to the house. But perhaps my mum was like that because my grandmother was strict. When we used to go and stay with her in Nigeria in the holidays, she was a tartar. Everything in its place. My mum was probably rebelling.

Do you feel like doing that with Rosie now?

Occasionally. If it gets so that I feel I can't breathe without her tensing up and thinking I'm making a mess, I'll just put things down exactly where I want to. Rosie always wants things put away immediately, or replaced exactly where she's put them. Sometimes it gets too much, even though I feel sorry for her. However careful I am, she'll usually adjust whatever it is – a cup, whatever – even if it's only by a millimetre.

What happens if you're untidy?

If it's a bad day, like Rosie's late for something, she'll burst into tears or say something really horrible. She always apologizes afterwards. I try not to get wound up: I know it's the OCD.

How long has Rosie had it?

Over fourteen years. I know because we were married fifteen years ago, and a few months after our wedding I realized something was wrong. Rosie hoovered and cleaned even more; she began worrying about tidiness all the time. We found out it was OCD through our GP.

Is she obsessive about anything else?

Yes, she worries all the time. My wife agonizes about what people think of her, she panics about whether the cat will return when she lets it out in the morning, she worries when I'm driving…

How's she coping with all the anxiety?

Not very well. Every day, I try to help and reassure her.

How are you coping yourself?

By remembering that OCD's not her fault. I respect Rosie; she does admit there's a problem. She's trying to fight the OCD. I make an effort to keep calm and have my own time too, where possible. I never pressurize Rosie if I can help it – say if we're in danger of running late – it just makes the rituals worse. She'll get tearful and refuse to go out at all, or the rituals last even longer. This can be really stressful for everyone. There've been plenty of times when I and other members of the family have waited outside in the car for her.

Has the illness changed your relationship?

Rosie's more distant from me now; she often seems to be in her own world.

What do the other members of your family think? Do they know about the OCD?

They don't know Rosie has it, although I think they suspect. She doesn't want people to know. But it makes things difficult because she wants the house very clean and tidy all the time, which isn't always possible.

Have other people been supportive, or are they not aware of it?

A couple of friends know about Rosie and they've been OK, but a lot of people don't know what OCD is.

Was it difficult for you at the beginning, getting information about it?

Yes. I wish someone had told me back then how best to cope with OCD. I've just found things out through experience.

Is Rosie on medication?

Yes, sertraline. Perhaps it takes the edge off the symptoms. Cognitive Behavioural Therapy (CBT) didn't work for her.

What about exposure to her fears, with a therapist?

She tried that too; that's what I mean about why I respect her.

Did it help at all?

No. Nothing really seems to help. I've begun going to a carers' support group. The only problem with that is that it's a long way for me to travel to the meetings; there isn't a local one. It's really helpful, though. I can talk freely, without watching what I'm saying in case it upsets my wife. It can be like treading on eggshells at home. The other people at the group understand, so you don't feel disloyal. Some of them are going through much worse: you get some perspective on things.

What does Rosie think about you attending the group?

Actually she suggested it, which surprised me, but it's really good she did. That's what I mean about her trying to fight the OCD. She began attending a group for people with OCD, about six months ago. Now Rosie will talk about the OCD as something separate – as in, "That's an OCD thought. I'm now going to sit down and watch a bit of TV, instead of cleaning." She still restricts what she eats, though, and won't try anything new. Exercise helps her de-stress. It definitely helps me – I really enjoy walking.

As we're saying goodbye, Jeremy says suddenly:

"I love Rosie to bits."

....

Fear of contamination can put an enormous strain on relationships. Divorce and separation rates are extremely high for people affected by this disorder. They are among the highest of any group with psychological or psychiatric problems. This may be because, should an OCD obsession centre on contamination from bodily products, it's fairly common to find associated sexual problems. There are patients, for example, who link contamination with seminal fluid. Others may demand that they and their partner are extremely clean, with washing and cleaning rituals before and after intercourse. To avoid perceived contamination, some people with OCD will insist that sex only takes place in a particular part of one room. Reassuringly, however, in the majority of cases, OCD doesn't necessarily impede the patient's sex life.

It appears that more females than males have the OCD "contamination" problem and carry out excessive cleansing. There are various reasons given for this, but often it's to dispose of dirt or germs.

....

Case study: Audrey

It was a crisis: my nine-year-old daughter refused to lie down; she said the bed was dirty. Sarah hadn't slept for forty-eight hours and was walking on tiptoe, her arms in the air. Her anxiety levels were sky high. The doctor said she should not have to wait to be assessed and Sarah was seen the next day. She was diagnosed with OCD.

The thing that had appeared to trigger it was a visit to the Imperial War Museum. We went on a visit to the trenches in the First World War installation – Sarah wanted to see it. They make the experience very realistic and I think it was the smell that set her off and all the dirt, with her passion for cleanliness. My daughter was horrified by the stench and asked what it was composed of. She couldn't get over the fact that the soldiers lived outside, under the sky in muddy trenches.

Sarah is now twenty, the youngest of my three girls. I had thought she might be autistic like her older sister, as she was stony-faced. She often laughed, but it didn't seem genuine. She was very particular about her clothes too, but I didn't think anything of it – after all, lots of people are interested in clothes, including me. I didn't know my daughter had OCD – in fact, when the doctor told me, I said, "What's that?" Once she explained, I realized I had heard of the condition before.

With hindsight, Sarah's grandmother might have had some OCD: we used to joke about her idiosyncrasies in the family. The cord had to be wound round the vacuum cleaner a set number of times after use, for no reason. She also refused point-blank to wear anything green – things like that.

I was dreading Sarah going on to secondary school, a big London comprehensive, after having had a good rapport with the teaching staff at her primary school. After almost a year of refusing to give Sarah medication, I capitulated – now I wonder why on earth we didn't let it happen immediately. It took a bit of time to find the right medication for her: sertraline didn't work; it made her mentally very unstable. This culminated in my daughter being found standing on a table crowing like a cockerel. She was out of her mind.

Her head of tutor group was utterly non-supportive. Things did get turned round: Sarah had different, successful, medication. She changed tutor groups. Her new head of tutor group/head of year was lovely, really supportive, as was her special needs support lady. They even attended our therapy sessions to better understand Sarah's needs.

In the second year, my daughter said she'd like to go on an Outward Bound course, which was facing her fears head on. She still had this horror of contamination. There were two girlfriends going and they said they'd look after her. Sarah said it was the worst week of her life. On the evening of the first day, we returned home to a heart-rending message on the answerphone. After a sleepless night, I rang the teacher the next morning to check – to my relief everything was OK.

With the right medication, Sarah gained awards at school and went on to get nine A–C GCSEs. Most importantly, she had good friends at this time. Unfortunately, she then dropped out of five A-levels she was doing, because she couldn't get organized.

Being a perfectionist, Sarah would rather not do things at all than do them badly.

She is so terrified of people being nasty to her that it only takes something small to upset her. She's a gifted dancer, but she won't attend classes since a girl said to her at the beginning of the second session: "Oh, it's you again." "So someone said 'Boo!' to you – just try to ignore it, Sarah," I say, but it doesn't work. She's done all the activities – singing, swimming, karate – until someone goes "Boo!" Then my daughter gives up.

Sarah can't use the landline phone at the moment. She's too frightened of someone being horrible to her, or of saying the wrong thing herself. She is depressed, though she can be good at hiding this, and has low self-esteem. My daughter is desperate to be liked, but in many ways she is immature and childlike, so it can be hazardous. I discovered she was giving her mobile number to complete strangers, just being friendly. We had to speak to these "callers" and threaten to call the police if they didn't stop ringing Sarah. The calls were often of a sexual nature – awful!

Sarah's still living at home and doing nothing with her life. We live in a four-bedroom, end of terrace house, so at least there's plenty of room. She's having a bad time at the moment, but coping better than she used to. Cognitive Behavioural Therapy (CBT) helps, but there's too much avoidance going on. Sarah insists she does do things but, as we discuss together, avoidance of potentially challenging situations is not overcoming OCD. She quite often sorts the dirty washing now, which she didn't used to be able to do.

I've lost friends through Sarah's illness. Some, I'm sure, get bored, because I don't get the chance to do much else at the moment so have little else to talk about. Some friends understand OCD, some don't; they just think Sarah's being naughty. She's not. It would be hard to reprimand Sarah, even if there was cause, without lowering her precarious self-esteem. Walking on eggshells here! The friends who've stayed the course are very supportive.

My husband and I take it in turns to stay at home. I work part-time so that Sarah and her autistic sister aren't left alone too much together, as then their anxieties multiply. Actually this sister has been trying to help by drawing up organizational charts to motivate her sister, but when Sarah doesn't act on them she is furious and gets upset.

Sarah is an angry young woman. When she was a child, I made her a cushion – I'm an artist and I work with textiles – with a picture of OCD on it which I'd copied from a drawing Sarah did. We encouraged her to kick this cushion, "kicking away the OCD" and to throw it around. More recently I've bought her a punchbag, which she finds useful to manage her anger.

Not long ago, Sarah had a boyfriend for about eight months. He was mad about her and wanted to get married. She dropped him; she couldn't get intimate.

Sarah currently has a great mental health team. The occupational therapist has found her two days of voluntary work a week, starting soon, which Sarah is apprehensive about. My daughter also gets Mobility Allowance of £34 per week, which at least means she has some money.

We eat very healthily, but Sarah didn't take any exercise at all last year. This week she attended a meditation and relaxation class – because I told her to take two of her Propranolol and dragged her there – and she loved it. The other people there had mental health problems, though not OCD, but it worked out well. Sarah's also on Prozac at the moment. She's attending weekly anxiety management sessions, with a good psychologist whom she trusts.

A while ago, for exercise and to help me cope, I took up running with a friend. It became more and more difficult to cover the distance. I was then diagnosed with a dangerously low blood count: this has affected my bones. I believe this is due to the long periods of stress I've had.

Last November I found out about the OCD Action Conference and went with Sarah. It was brilliant and my daughter stayed the whole day – against all the odds. I wouldn't want to set up an OCD support group, though, as was suggested in one of the sessions: I just want a life away from it. For me, studying [as a mature student] has been the focus outside a home life that has, at different times, been hell. Thank God for art; it has been so cathartic.

....

Interview: Marjorie

Christopher's father, Robin, and I had never heard of OCD when our son began manifesting strange facial tics. They'd happen after a traumatic event and were accompanied by night terrors and sleepwalking. The event which set all this off was when Chris, aged two and a half, went to look closely at the head of George Bernard Shaw in a waxwork museum. He was fascinated by it. The effigy was high inside a glass case, rotating on a string, so his father had to lift Chris up so he could see it more closely. Suddenly a long white waxwork hand, dripping blood, shot up in front of Chris's face. Our son literally turned blue with shock.

After this, Chris used to wash his hands constantly; he was terrified of anything to do with hands. This applied if he saw them in shop windows on the mannequins, on TV, appearing from behind curtains – anywhere. At night, he would have nightmares in which he'd see hands in the curtains. Chris started to vomit every morning before going to school. He developed a nervous blink, followed by an all-subsuming facial tic. Chris was teased and bullied at school because of this. Luckily teachers were very helpful, although staff at the school had no idea what was wrong with him.

As a psychotherapist, and prior to that, it never occurred to me that what Chris was suffering was in any way his fault. Some of my family, namely my parents, thought it was most definitely all my fault. They made my life a misery, in particular my mother. Since this was projected onto me, though, my son remained *very fond of them and has good memories of his grandparents. Thankfully my relationship with others hasn't been affected by the OCD: my sister and brother-in-law are very understanding, as are other friends and relatives.*

My relationship with my son has not really altered over the years due to OCD: it would seem he's always had it in one form or another. Certainly we have a very good rapport now. He also gets on well with his sister, who is a teacher, his father, my three grandchildren and also his aunt and uncle. Chris relates well to family friends, but likes his own company.

I suppose I wish someone could have told me what was wrong with my son earlier, but back then no one knew. I found it initially very difficult to get information about OCD. No one forty years ago had heard of it. It was only when I spotted a book in Cambridge called The Boy Who Couldn't Stop Washing *that I first had an inkling of what it was. Now I look everywhere for information on OCD: libraries, online forums, I speak to doctors, and so on. Our family doctor is extremely helpful. I also sometimes attend a local carers' support group. Chris has had help from the local carers' group; he worked with an excellent young carer with loads of ideas, intellect and character. It's good that the group exists.*

Normally, Chris's choice of treatment is avoidance. People have tried to be helpful, but he's refused any assistance. This has been the most difficult and frustrating part of all. He is a strong character and very resistant to aid, but is glad when he manages to agree to it. My son wouldn't speak about any of his feelings or thoughts – he was in complete denial – for many years. Then, a few weeks ago, Chris attended his first [Stevenage] OCD Sufferers' Group session, forty-plus years after the original traumatic event.

FEAR OF ILLNESS

Fear of illness is linked to anxieties about contamination. Instead of worrying about causing harm to other people through germs, the anxiety is turned inward onto the OCD sufferer.

Because of fear of contracting germs from other people, the person with OCD might avoid:[2]

- using public toilets
- shaking hands
- touching door knobs/handles
- using public telephones
- waiting in a GP's surgery
- visiting hospitals
- eating in a café/restaurant
- washing clothes in a launderette
- touching banisters on staircases
- touching poles
- being in a crowd.

You might also notice the person:

- avoiding red objects and stains, due to their anxiety about contracting HIV/AIDS from blood-like stains
- shaking clothes excessively, to remove dead skin cells
- brushing their teeth too much, due to worry about missing minute particles of mouth disease
- avoiding coming into contact with chemicals.

....

Interview: Rebecca

Mum's OCD was triggered by her developing pre-skin cancer on her face. It was mad – just the mention of the word "cancer" sent her into a whirlwind of mind-blowing OCD, even though it was "pre-cancerous".

Some people are very frightened of cancer, though.

Yes, sure – I think the connection of cancer fear here is Mum's memories of her mother's horrific death from it. It was back in 1958 – it's something she's never got over. My mum is seventy-nine now. Looking back, she's had OCD probably most of her life, but it's got much worse in the last ten years; the doctor diagnosed it.

Does your mother carry out any rituals?

She has rituals every day: morning washing and dressing can take three hours, before she even comes downstairs. Mum has a different pair of slippers for the bathroom and the kitchen and so on. If she's emptying her bowel – her most feared ritual and our most natural one – she could take five hours, because of the cleanliness battle.

How is your mother at meal times?

She uses her own crockery, her own cutlery, her glass… They are all marked with nail varnish, so everyone knows not to touch them. Mum washes her hands constantly with Dettol. She wears rubber gloves daily.

What, all the time?

Well, if she isn't wearing them, she'll turn lights off with her elbow. She won't touch a telephone, because someone's breathed into it. She can't mail a letter as she won't go outside into "contaminated" air. We never go out together; she won't visit my house. There are many more things.

Do you know if your mum also obsessively worries about issues – maybe without rituals?

Yes. The slightest thing will send her into a frantic worry; she will hysterically cry until the small problem has been solved by my father or me. We have lied to calm her down.

Are you able to take holidays?

She used to come on holiday with me and my family, but she'd beg me beforehand to clean the bathroom and kitchen of the room/caravan/villa we were staying in. She won't ever go on holiday again, though. She won't sit on public transport, or sleep in "someone else's bed".

What is her home like?

She and my dad have a very nice three-bedroom house, but she won't allow anybody except me, my sister and our children inside. Mum is so paranoid. If there's a knock on the door, she hides and cries. My dad is forbidden to answer his own front door. It's very stressful visiting them. Their home smells of Dettol and she has plastic bags on most of the chairs. There's a bag on the door to catch mail – and Mum won't use the washing machine. She says it's too dirty. She also forbids me to see some relatives, as they've had cancer. She thinks it's catching.

Isn't she relieved by the fact they've survived? So if she did get cancer, she might live too?

I don't know – it doesn't seem to make a difference at the moment. Family members are very sad for her, but as she refuses any help from them and won't discuss it, they are turning bitter. They miss seeing my dad, their brother.

How does your father cope?

Not very well, but he tries his best for a peaceful life. He is a 79-year-old man who loves his wife unconditionally, but he is tired from the effort he makes every day to keep her happy. The way I cope is by my dad telling me that OCD is no one's fault, and by using a lot of patience. Although she's still my loving mother, I feel I have lost her to demons.

We sit in silence for a moment.

It's how Mum describes what's inside her.

Was it difficult for you finding out about OCD when your mother was diagnosed?

No, the doctor was great; Mum only saw him once or twice, though. She refuses to take medication. She says drugs are bad and will lead to cancer; she has not been near a doctor or a hospital for nine years. My father and I have tried talking to her about herbal treatments, but my mother refuses to try anything. Years ago, she did have phone counselling once, but said the lady had no sympathy and refused to speak to her again. The doctor's not allowed in, of course. Even he asked what more he could do. My dad and I look up information about OCD online, but her case is so extreme there's nothing more to do than to live out their days like this. My dad doesn't attend a support group. I think he'd love support and some respite, but she wouldn't let him go to anything like that. We talk to each other when my mother's asleep. If she thought I was talking to you now, she'd be livid.

Have you had support from any other people?

Yes, most people are understanding when I say it is a mental illness. I find chocolate helps me through it – and long walks with the dog. I wish Mum would do some exercise, but she doesn't do any. If anyone else has discovered someone they love has OCD, I'd say do not be soft with them. Be strong. Fight that devil inside their mind. It is a battle of wills. My dad gives in to my mum too much, for a peaceful life.

FEAR OF HARMING OTHERS

OCD sufferers often live in terror of something catastrophic happening, and see themselves as responsible for it not occurring. Common fears revolve around fire, burglary or flooding. Irons, cookers, locks and taps in the home therefore can easily become the focus of OCD anxiety, and in their anxiety people with OCD may turn taps off too hard, for example. Another fear, that of the death of loved ones, might make it difficult for a person with OCD to go to bed at night. What if a fire flared up once everyone was asleep?

CHECKING

Someone with OCD will often feel comforted when carrying out repetitive checking rituals. These rituals are to try to control their environment and ensure that everyone's safe. Checking may be manifested in the following ways:

- verifying that the sufferer hasn't or will not harm others

- checking that they haven't or won't harm themselves

- establishing that nothing terrible has happened

- testing that they haven't made a mistake (despite exhaustive efforts not to)

- checking some aspect of their health or body.

....

Interview: Barbara's friend, Esther

My friend, Esther, constantly inspects her home before going out. It can take up to half an hour. She looks to see whether plugs, taps, cooker and the iron are switched off. The fridge door is tapped several times – I guess to see whether it is closed properly. Locks on all the windows and the front door are checked several times, to ensure the house is burglar-proof. Esther's other OCD thing is continually washing, especially her hands. I feel sorry for her; I wish I was able to help more. She worries all the time; she never feels good enough. She is always anxious and says other people don't understand. She often feels "got at".

She has had OCD for at least twenty years, possibly longer. She only told me a couple of years ago, though – even though we've been good friends for thirty-five years! I get the impression that illness brought on her OCD.

I've noticed that her symptoms seem to come and go in episodes, depending on how much stress there is to deal with. But the OCD is always in the background. I can cope with my friend's behaviour and it helps that I have a bit of an understanding of OCD. Because I'm a counsellor, I have been able to access information for her. Esther has been given leaflets too by her female GP, whom she says is very understanding. I try to support my friend as much as possible. We discussed her routine before leaving the house and I made it into a checklist. Once windows, doors, plugs have been checked once, they get ticked off on the chart. It now only takes a few minutes for Esther to leave the house. This has been very helpful, especially for her getting to work on time.

Her husband, Mark, left her just over a year ago; the divorce is going through now. It's a shame I haven't been able to persuade Esther to go on holiday somewhere, to relax and have some fun. She finds it too difficult to stay away from home, though, especially for any length of time. Perhaps she will think about attending a support group, but up until now my friend has tended to keep the fact she has OCD to herself, as much as possible. She worries that others won't understand. She's lacked the confidence to try CBT too.

She has been bullied in the past, both at work and at home, which made her turn to comfort eating. For the past ten years or so, she has been very overweight and also in pain from arthritis, *but things are improving. She is eating more healthily now and has lost quite a lot of weight. We invite each other over for dinner and cook a really nice (low calorie) meal every couple of weeks or so.*

Esther was on anti-depressants and anti-inflammatory medication; I'm not sure what the situation is at present. At one point she had a couple of sessions with a clinical psychologist, but she told me it wasn't particularly successful. I personally think CBT would be a good idea.

....

We see this hyper-responsible feeling extending to a fear of harming others, due to not being sufficiently careful. The thoughts of a person with OCD might run something like this: "What if I drop something on the ground or leave this stone on the pavement and someone slips and hurts themselves? It'll be my fault. I now feel tempted to drop something on the ground, but I mustn't. What a bad person I am." These excoriating thoughts run on a relentless loop, upping the individual's panic and guilt. For instance: Isobel obsessively worries about harm coming to her family. Her chief fears seem to be of burglary and fire. She is terrified that candles will spontaneously combust and burn the house down, so if she discovers any in the family home, she will put them in her handbag and take them out with her. When asked whether she doesn't worry that they will spontaneously combust in her handbag, it appears that the lack of logic in her action hadn't occurred to her, nor did it seem to make her fear that this would happen. It is injury to her family or damage to her home that seems to consume her. The candles don't seem to have the same power once removed from that environment.

Someone with OCD might also mentally review events. They will keep checking their memory, endeavouring to prevent harm to themselves or others, or to avert horrific consequences.

A therapist says

> One of my patients has obsessive thoughts about her
> parents dying. She feels compelled to repeat certain
> behaviours to prevent this happening.

....

Interview: Dorothy, a mother

*My 22-year-old son, Ryan, obsesses about the death of people
close to him. It began with the death of a baby, mine, when
Ryan was four and a half. OCD was then triggered big time by
a series of family deaths when my son was fourteen. Ryan's pet
rabbit also died around the same time and this tipped him into
full-on OCD.*

*My son also worries about getting older. As well as this, he
has Body Dysmorphic Disorder (BDD) and is very concerned
about his appearance, particularly his ears. At home, Ryan
struggles with "thresholds", so he hesitates before walking through
doorways. He mutters things while eating and leaves particular
types of food on his plate – he refuses to eat certain ingredients.
Ryan often holds two fingers together, or fiddles with his nose.
He looks at his penis frequently when he's anxious, as he has
paedophile anxieties.*

*I have low-impact OCD myself and am a counsellor, which
helped me to recognize OCD in my son. My relationship with
him has altered since his early teens: there is a lot more tension
between us now. A person with OCD is more disconnected.
Ryan and I still share the same sense of humour, though, which
helps a lot. In other ways his condition has brought the family
closer together. My daughter and other son get on better, and my
husband and I have a stronger relationship now – we are united
in a common front against OCD taking over. My daughter has
hardly reacted to her brother's illness: she's not really that bothered.
She just moves on with her own life. The only time it impinges*

is when my son has really bad OCD, when she is embarrassed to invite friends home. She's mainly away at university now, so it's not a problem for her. My youngest son, though, has been very angry with his older brother and jealous of the attention (he perceives) he gets from me.

Ryan hasn't experienced any discrimination or bullying: he's very open about his OCD and has loads of friends; he's very popular. I've encouraged him to lead as normal a life as he can. He's coping OK-ish at uni. He's on a placement year at the moment and living at home, so the OCD is not impacting him as much as when he's living away. His school was very good and so is his university. They give him extensions on his work deadlines when the OCD is bad.

As a family, we've always gone on holiday together, but a couple have been a nightmare. This is due to the struggle when leaving places. Ryan is scared that he "might not leave them right" and can spend all day trying to leave a mobile home on the last day of the break.

I didn't have a problem initially finding out about OCD, but it was very difficult accessing correct and consistent aid. I look on the web for information at present, and our doctor is very helpful. Other people have been reasonably supportive.

I believe that changes in diet for those with OCD can be very useful — although it's difficult to persuade my son of that. Ryan would love to live on alcohol, pizzas and chocolate. I try to persuade him to eat fruit and vegetables daily when he's away at uni. I have a friend who is a nutritional therapist, who compiled information for me relating to OCD and diet. While he's at home, Ryan's OCD is noticeably better because he's eating very healthily and taking his medication regularly.

Ryan is on fluoxetine, which works well for him — as does exercise. CBT works for him too, when he engages with it. I so wish my son had had CBT earlier: it took ages to obtain help for him. It wasn't the doctor's fault; just that the local CAMHS

(Child and Adolescent Mental Health Services) weren't very good or helpful. I think exposure to his fears with a therapist worked for Ryan, but he easily slips back into the intrusive thoughts after a while.

I've found it doesn't help me to eat lots of chocolate or sugar. Talking to friends, socializing and having a sense of humour relieves the pressure. I also run local OCD support groups in Hertfordshire. I've been doing this for about three years.

....

REPETITIVE ACTION RITUALS

People with OCD often spend time unnecessarily repeating actions in an attempt to feel secure. However, these may be activities totally unrelated to what's happening around the person at the time. An individual could carry out a task five times, for example, because five is associated in their mind with being the "right" number to help control the anxiety. They might hoover the rug in five-movement batches, for example, or pick up a bag and put it down five times. Someone with this type of OCD compulsion might duplicate movements such as tapping, touching or avoiding touching things; they might also blink too often. The person could also "forensically" inspect written matter, or rewrite something seemingly unnecessarily, to ease their inner panic. Obviously though, repetitive actions will depend on context:

> *Q: When is arranging DVDs neatly for eight hours a day not a compulsion?*

> *A: When a person works in a music store.*[3]

....

Interview: Erica

Bryony is my stepdaughter. She used to straighten all the shoes on the back porch before entering the house. This could take up to an hour to get them exact. She repeated almost all actions four times. She would tap items four times. Take four drinks of water at a time. She would reread everything four times. If she saw a word on a sign, she'd have to look at the sign four separate times. She had to leave things exactly as she found them.

She stopped touching almost everything, in case she messed something up. She walked around with her arms flat against her sides, to be sure she didn't touch anything in a store. She repeated words or sentences four times. She was obsessed with leaves and sticks in the yard. She would spend hours picking up each and every leaf she saw. Finally, she got to the point where she would not look out of windows, and hid on the floor of the car when we drove in or out of the driveway, so she did not see the yard at all.

Bryony's now aged fifteen. She was ten when the OCD was at its worst and she was diagnosed. I had already done Internet research and could clearly tell her symptoms matched those for OCD. I'm sure Bryony was born with it: I can look back and see she had signs of OCD from the age of two. It became increasingly worse from when she was about eight. The OCD became full-blown and we had to seek treatment when Bryony's biological mother gave birth to another baby, and her grandfather, whom Bryony was extremely close to, died. Both events happened within a month of each other.

She worried about things. She was convinced she would be kidnapped. We don't stand out from other people: we live in an upper-middle class suburb [of a large American city], but it didn't reassure her. Bryony spent two years thinking of little else other than when and where she would be kidnapped. My daughter also obsessed for about nine months over what time she would fall asleep. She was afraid she would be awake all night. Literally as soon as she woke in the morning, she would start talking about how and when she would fall asleep the coming night.

The other main thought obsession is of going to jail. They went on a field-trip in fifth grade to the police station. She has been terrified that she will go to jail ever since. She used to be afraid that she had shoplifted something when she really hadn't. She is drawn to the news and TV shows and movies that are based in jail. She wants to see everything about it.

Happily, today, my daughter is coping well. Almost all her rituals and thoughts are gone. For me, I only sought support from people that I knew would be supportive – if that makes sense. I found the Yahoo online OCD and parenting support groups extremely helpful: they were a wealth of information. I also discovered other people that understood the disease, whom I could talk to. I tried to keep our lives on track and made a big effort not to accommodate the obsessions. I ignored Bryony's compulsions as much as possible and just forged on with life. Our doctor was not terribly helpful, but we did find a good therapist, through word of mouth. I wish someone had told me earlier that with medicine and/or Exposure and Response Prevention (ERP) and/or education, things can improve dramatically.

Bryony is who she is, and I am who I am. I can't separate her from the disease. Our relationship today, being mother and teen, compared to our relationship when she was younger – mother and child/pre-teen – is different. But it would have changed with or without OCD, I think.

My relationship with family members and colleagues has altered. When the OCD was at its worst, I was withdrawn from family and co-workers. OCD is exhausting and if people don't understand it, it's too difficult to describe. Also, my daughter was extremely embarrassed by her own behaviour and the diagnosis. She did not want me discussing it with others. Out of respect for her, I honoured her wishes. So when we were deep in the trenches, OCD was very isolating for our entire family. She also almost completely withdrew from all of her friends at that time. Her friends' parents are my friends, so I missed those relationships and "play-dates". As much as possible, we did not alter our home, or reschedule our holidays. We took the stance that we were not going to adapt to OCD; rather OCD had to adapt to us. That was so much more difficult than you can imagine.

My fifth-grade daughter vomited her breakfast every morning because of nerves. For two months she went into school shaking and crying with fear and anxiety, but I was not going to stop serving breakfast every morning, and I was not going to hold her out of school. I felt like if I gave OCD one inch, it would swallow my daughter and I would never get her back. Some parents take a different approach. I think every mother has to know her own child and do what she feels is best.

Bryony's sister is eighteen months older. She does not have OCD. She and her father found it frustrating and I don't think they understood as well as I did. They did not do the research and make the connections I did. I think they thought a lot of it was for attention, or that Bryony should just be able to stop the behaviour. We are extremely blessed that she got to go to a great school. Although most kids and teachers did not know what she was struggling with, they were still generally sympathetic. I hadn't really thought about it until now, but we were very lucky she was not singled out or bullied. Our school system has been somewhat accommodating to her. As far as possible, we've kept her completely on schedule. She has always completed all her homework on time, even though it involved hours of erasing, and repeating, and rereading. She has gone to school every day and has participated in all activities, no matter how uncomfortable for her. But they did let her go to the nurse's office when she was feeling overwhelmed occasionally.

4

Hoarding
. . . .

Hoarding is the practice of collecting items resulting in significant clutter in the home.[1] It was a hidden disorder until research on it picked up in the early 1990s. Since then, interest has increased dramatically among research scientists and clinicians. Media coverage of hoarding has also increased public awareness.

. . . .

Interview: Damien, a friend of a hoarder

Mac is a single man, aged sixty-five, living alone in the semi-detached family house. He was an only child; he hasn't any immediate relatives alive now to my knowledge. His hoarding consists of material specifically relating to historical research — books and documents in the main. Despite the house being full to bursting, he has not cleared any rooms of furniture, clothes and effects belonging to his late parents. These are all still in place, surrounded by boxes of research material. Not exactly hoarding, but suggesting a difficulty in being able to move on.

Neither has my friend apparently done any house cleaning except in the kitchen which, though very dated, is reasonably clean and tidy. Elsewhere, most objects on mantelpieces and so on lie under a deep layer of dust. The stuff hasn't been touched for years, maybe even decades. Though Mac says he'd like some help to sort things out, he can't decide where to start or where to put the stuff while sorting. It would be a very daunting task for anyone to try to help with, as he's unlikely to allow anything to be touched or moved without a great deal of "negotiation".

I only realized my friend was a hoarder when I was invited to his house for the first time – after more than thirty years. Mac has apparently hoarded things for several decades. Before that he had a troubled childhood and felt excluded at school. Bullying was a major factor there. Mac has told me he used to run away and hide at break-times, so I think this must have had a very damaging effect at a crucial stage in his development – a point he makes himself. These experiences have become an obsession with him.

So Mac's house is jammed full of boxes of books, magazines and other documents relating to historical research. This has now become his lifetime's (unpaid) work. He doesn't have anyone else to think about, so his day revolves around this occupation to the exclusion of almost everything else. Mac hasn't worked outside the home for about thirty years, but he isn't financially hard up so can get by. I estimate that the house has had no maintenance, at least since his mother died about ten years ago. The place hasn't been cleaned for so long because Mac doesn't see that as a priority. Nor does he try to manage the hoarded items more efficiently – again this would be a distraction from the main task of research. He feels too that there is no one to help him get on top of things.

We only speak occasionally, maybe three or four times a year. Our conversations are usually 99 per cent him talking, which I believe is what he needs to do. Each time we speak he relates the experiences of his early childhood, how these damaged his development and how no one can help him to move forward. I feel sorry for Mac, wrestling constantly with the torment of his past, but it can get frustrating. He won't allow anyone to take charge in a practical sense, like maybe clearing the house. I think changes in diet or exercise patterns might prove very useful for him too. The problem is "enforcing" these things when the person concerned lives alone. He doesn't respond well to advice anyway, always tending to challenge it. Least likely thing for Mac to say? "Mmm, I think you're right."

Mac has isolated himself and no one visits him (excepting my visit last year). However, he does communicate with friends by phone and email and will occasionally meet them away from the house. He looks after his appearance, and meeting him, you wouldn't know his living conditions are so dire. He never takes holidays, but he occasionally takes trips abroad to further his research. He meets people there whom he's conversed with by phone or email.

Mac has told doctors about his problems many times, but hoarding is only one of the issues. It's a symptom, like leaving the house uncleaned for years is. Most of the experts who have seen him seem to have come to the conclusion that his case is too complex and cannot be solved. He himself has written a long and detailed "report" on his life to save time explaining everything again to each new professional. He says his predicament results from: strict parenting, being an only child, never having received love from his mother and having a very disciplinarian father.

A woman he saw for a few sessions last year did seem to be making some progress (which may have been why he finally allowed me to visit him) but I think it came to an end. Since then the situation has not improved. I've not heard of anyone giving him day-to-day support. Mac does have an old school friend who supported him in the past, but he's now very ill.

....

Feedback from friends of people who hoard

> I believe it's a symptom — try to find the root cause.
> It could be low self-esteem, loneliness or feelings of
> rejection.
> **James**

Changes in diet and exercise would probably be very useful for him. My friend doesn't exercise at all and, although he's a good cook, he has a bad diet. He just can't see the point of making an effort. There is clearly a depression element to this.
Luke

My friend has very low self-esteem and his method of coping with this is the acquisition of more things. This provides temporary relief – a short-term fix, like "retail therapy".
Judith

Try to get the person to talk about how they feel to anyone they feel comfortable with and take it from there.
Oli

A SEPARATE CONDITION?

Compulsive hoarding is a widely recognized symptom of OCD, although there are moves afoot to make it a separate condition. Hoarding is not currently considered an illness in its own right, but this is due to change. In the USA, hoarding is being considered for inclusion in DSM-5, in May 2013. (The planned fifth edition of the American Psychiatric Association's *Diagnostic and Statistical Manual of Mental Disorders*.) Compulsive hoarding is then expected to be defined as a distinct disorder, rather than as a symptom of OCD.

While there are several ways in which hoarding resembles OCD, there are many ways in which it appears quite distinct. Similarities between hoarding and OCD include:[2]

- fears of losing important information

- fears of losing objects of emotional significance

- fears of making serious mistakes

- concern with symmetry

- distress when others touch or move the owner's possessions

- feelings of guilt.

Differences include:

- the thoughts of a hoarder not being intrusive, repetitive or distressing

- no rituals

- hoarding thoughts more often resemble preoccupations than obsessions

- when getting rid of possessions the hoarder is likely to experience grief or anger as much as anxiety

- a hoarder considers their behaviour to be normal ("ego syntonic"); "What if I should need it in future?" tends to be their rationale

- a person with OCD considers their symptoms to be "ego dystonic" or inconsistent with normal behaviour and their sense of self

- hoarding is often associated with positive experiences, even euphoria – emotions almost unknown in OCD.

There are five features which categorize people with hoarding OCD:[3]

1. *Indecisiveness* – this appears to be related to the perfectionist fear of making mistakes. Hoarding useless objects could be a means of avoiding making decisions that may be regretted later if they lose or discard something they then wish they'd kept.

2. *Problems with categorization* – people with hoarding OCD have difficulty classifying objects for efficient use, or throwing away. One thing seems as important as another. There is an inability to differentiate between what is really valuable and what isn't.

3. *Beliefs about memory* – individuals with hoarding OCD often display obsessional concern about the reliability of their memory. An accompanying lack of confidence in their faulty memory makes them reluctant to put items away. They fear that if the object is out of sight, it will be forgotten. This leads to cluttered surroundings.

4. *Excessive emotional attachment to things* – people with hoarding OCD regard their stuff as part of themselves. They experience great emotional comfort (Frost and Gross, 1993[4]) from their possessions, much more than non-hoarders do. This often results in excessive purchasing, or shopaholic behaviour.

5. *Control of ownership* – the owner needs to feel completely in control of their possessions, to protect the items from irresponsible use or harm. They will feel extreme discomfort should their objects be touched by anyone else.

Some researchers think compulsive hoarding is almost always an independent condition, but often found in conjunction/co-morbidity with other psychological disorders.

....

Interview: Susan, a mother

My son Ade has suffered greatly with depression and anxiety, but fortunately has always loved reading. He is interested in history, travel, ancient buildings and foreign travel, and this gives him some pleasure. Ade's hoarding remains a problem and a challenge. He is due to move into a large house with Richard, his father, fairly soon. Ade, at forty-five, doesn't live in his house but currently with me, or with Richard. All three houses are full of my son's hoards.

Comfort eating is sometimes a problem for Ade: since taking drugs prescribed by the specialist, he has put on weight. The medication works to a degree; I don't know what type he is on. His father knows, but I've not been involved in this and don't want to ask him.

When my son is willing to do it, exercise proves useful against the OCD. I also find exercise helpful, but have to be careful after a nasty broken ankle ten years ago which has never healed properly. My son hasn't tried CBT. He did attempt exposure to his fears briefly with a therapist, but it was unsuccessful. It involved trying to pack up his things to move house, but Ade found them all "contaminated", so the problem remains.

....

Interview: Jo, a friend of a hoarder

Robert is a middle-aged man. He is in a relationship but doesn't live with his girlfriend. He is currently supporting an ageing aunt, staying with her as a carer. My friend has an older brother (they're not in contact) and cousins living elsewhere in the UK. Robert's hoarding over the past thirty years has consisted of the acquisition of books, tools and equipment. This is all to support a self-sufficient lifestyle in the country. For Robert this is a "means to an end" and his dream. But due to lack of capital, it's unlikely to happen anytime soon. He hasn't worked in paid employment for years.

My friend is very environmentally aware; he's totally averse to waste. This means that hardly anything gets thrown away. All used food packaging, milk containers and so on, is washed and retained. There are teetering heaps of stuff stacked everywhere. Robert's hoarding isn't limited to specific items to fulfil his dream, but has widened to include all potentially reusable objects.

He's very well read and has a great knowledge of mechanics, horticulture and building maintenance. He could easily work in any of these fields, except that he suffers from a complete lack of self-confidence and also hasn't found his "dream job".

I only realized that Robert had hoarding issues when his mother died. He had shared a flat with her and clearing the property took several weeks. I'd known him for over twenty years by then, but he'd never allowed me inside the flat before. It was quite a shock. A few months earlier, his brother had been in with his wife and done some sorting out and cleaning. Previously it had been worse even than what I saw. His collecting leads to hoarding and has a very narrowing effect on his life. The dream lifestyle he's harboured for years is an excuse for just acquiring more stuff.

There are plenty of things to pin the hoarding to in Robert's life: it's not been easy. Parental break-up; he has a distant relationship with his brother – there's a ten-year age difference. He's been through divorce, too, and is unable to hold down a job. My friend hates form-filling and won't claim benefits. He never approached social services for help with his mother either, supporting her himself. Life is currently very dull, but Robert does have skills for caring for others and he looks after his aunt very well. This repeats, in a sense, the fifteen years with his mother.

I call him at least once a week. When my friend lived nearby we used to go out for a drink and try to talk through the issues. I've found it very difficult to find useful information on hoarding. Robert has almost a hatred of professional "helpers", so he wouldn't be willing to cooperate with anything like that. He's also very dismissive of doctors and medication. He proudly boasts he hasn't seen a dentist for thirty years; he admired his great-aunt for pulling out her own teeth with a piece of string.

He has had a few short-term jobs. I wish I could provide the framework for realizing his big dream and get him into regular work. Being made to feel wanted for his skills and experience *would, I believe, greatly improve his mood. Without building the self-esteem that comes with joining the world of work, he's on a slow downward spiral. Unfortunately, when Robert is asked to do some work for someone, he prices his time absurdly low – while he tries really hard to do the very best job he can – such is his lack of self-worth. As a result he receives little more than the cost of materials. He complains about it afterwards, but says he would have lost the work to someone else if he'd charged more.*

Robert has completely cut himself off from his brother since his mother's flat was cleared. He sees his brother as not having done enough to support their mother, despite living nearby. He's had a lot of support from his girlfriend. She is very patient and understands a lot of what's going on, but their being apart geographically doesn't help.

....

TREATMENT

Treatment of hoarding is often a challenge and meets with mixed success. Many people who hoard don't recognize the negative impact of hoarding on their lives, or don't believe they need treatment. This is particularly true if their possessions, or animals, offer comfort. If these are removed, the hoarder will often quickly collect more to help to fulfil their emotional needs. Try to find a therapist or other mental health provider who has experience in treating hoarding. While therapy can be intense and time-consuming, it can pay off in the long run.

There are two main types of treatment for hoarding: psychotherapy and medication.[5]

CBT is the most common form of psychotherapy used to treat hoarding. As part of Cognitive Behavioural Therapy, the person with hoarding issues may:

- explore why they feel compelled to hoard

- learn to organize and categorize possessions, to help them decide which ones to discard

- improve their decision-making skills

- de-clutter their home during in-home visits by a therapist or professional organizer

- learn and practise relaxation skills

- attend family or group therapy

- be encouraged to consider psychiatric hospitalization if their hoarding is severe

- have periodic visits or ongoing treatment to help them to maintain healthy habits.

Research continues regarding the most effective ways to use medication in the treatment of hoarding. Types of medication most commonly used for hoarding are SSRIs, such as paroxetine (Paxil) – see page 90 for further information. However, not everyone responds to this treatment.

A therapist's view

> Hoarders should be encouraged to consider
> psychiatric hospitalization if their practice of
> hoarding is severe.
> **Robert Edge**

Simon's experience of living with a hoarder

Simon's wife has various OCD-related rituals, and is also a hoarder. Simon eventually thought he would throw away a couple of the many black bin bags set aside for checking by Victoria. They appeared to be crammed with items the family no longer required. He had difficulty extracting the bags from the under-stairs cupboard, they were so tightly jammed in with other sacks. While Victoria was bathing their child one evening, Simon surreptitiously crept out with two of the bags and took them to a large bin, half a mile away, to avoid detection. Victoria was not fooled for an instant: "Where's the bag with the cheese grater in? It was in the cupboard." Simon capitulated and admitted he'd thrown it away. The ensuing dissention persuaded him it wasn't worth it (until next time). He is full of sympathy and love for his wife. The relationship is also helped by the fact he respects Victoria for admitting she has a hoarding problem. He appreciates her ongoing efforts to deal with it.

It's funny; before we lived together, I never really noticed anything different about the way Vic lived. Sure, there were a few bags with stuff in, in a corner of her room, but I just vaguely thought she was having a clear-out. Now, it feels like every time I come home to our house, another bag has appeared. Last weekend, I got frustrated by it all and Victoria agreed she'd empty the kitchen cupboard. There's one above the sink, full of hundreds of little half-empty spice jars. We don't cook much. I came home from work all expectant yesterday, as she said she'd emptied the cupboard, but now I see that the jars are all stacked really neatly on the work-top by the sink. They haven't gone far. Vic thinks they look nice there. And the cupboards are full up again.

Simon shakes his head, laughing, but rueful.

....

Interview: Angela, niece of Annette

My aunt Annette was a lovely woman, really kind. I remember her as always immaculately turned out — no one ever guessed she was a hoarder and living in chaos. Annette had a large first-floor apartment in Dortmund, Germany. We saw each other about four times a year; I remember her flat being very messy but we didn't spend much time there when I visited. We would go out a lot, to restaurants and shows. Annette liked doing that and she was comfortably off. She didn't seem to mind the mess, but she never invited friends to her flat that I knew of. She'd always rather meet them at cafés or restaurants. I remember I used to surreptitiously check the use-by dates on food the few times we did eat at home, as she was vague about it. I did it secretly as it could cause a little tension with my aunt if I complained about food being unsafe, or if I tried to clean something. I didn't realize how bad things were on the hoarding front until Annette died, and I went over to Germany to sort out her estate single-handedly.

She must have been a hoarder for at least ten years. I found all the shelves, cupboards, sideboards, wardrobes – you name it – full to the brim with things. There were overflowing boxes all over the floor of the flat, into which Annette had stuffed extra items. There were ornaments and other objects piled high on furniture; you couldn't see the big dining table.

It was all very dirty. It would have been impossible to keep it clean, and Annette hadn't made any effort to. I knew she was never particularly tidy or into housework, but it was horrific. I found food in the kitchen cupboards which was a decade out of date. Tins had rusted right through the metal and were oozing stuff. Things were alive in the rubbish covering the floor; I was scared to death I'd see a rat. The freezer was almost as bad: there was six-year-old food stacked in there. Most of the stuff in the main fridge was months past its eat-by date.

I made innumerable visits to the dump with the car full of bin bags of smelly rubbish. I took the contents of a whole room full of shoes and clothes, once I could get in there, in batches to charity shops. Finally, after about a week of working hard clearing the flat, I thought I'd finished. I was about to lock up and leave, when I remembered Annette's cellar. It was in the basement of the block. I went downstairs and unlocked the door. I nearly cried. This large room was packed to the ceiling with more old food,

*newspapers, magazines, bottles and the like. My aunt could easily
have taken most of it to recycling facilities close by.*

*I began thinking about stressful events which might have set
off her behaviour. She wasn't always messy and accruing stuff.
Her brother died, though that was probably a bit later, after the
onset of her hoarding. Not long after that happened, the husband
of her best friend died. My aunt's friend lived downstairs in the
apartment block and Annette had to help her with shopping and
the like (her friend was disabled). Around the same time, she
had to take semi-retirement from her job, which she liked, then
a few years later, full retirement.*

*She would never have gone to a doctor about her problems.
I haven't looked up information on hoarding, so I don't know
about potential treatments. I wish I could have prevented the
mess from building up, but as I was living abroad and only
visiting, there was very little I could have done. There were no
other relatives who could have got involved.*

....

Interview: Christine, a friend of a hoarder

*Isabella's main issue is hoarding, but she also has intrusive
thoughts about harm coming to her family and is driven by the
need to protect them. She finds it impossible to accept that she
can't control everything. I originally met Isabella when she was
temporarily covering the role of Executive Assistant that I was
appointed to. We got to know each other during the handover
period. I told her about my own problems with OCD, as I am
quite open about this, and she gradually opened up about her
experiences. Isabella mentioned "wasting several years" of her
life on OCD, so I think she's had it since she was in her late
teens/early twenties. I believe Isabella lives in a house with her
parents and younger brother. I'm going on what she's told me,
as I've never visited her at home. Her brother has some kind
of undiagnosed behavioural problems – possibly on the autistic*

spectrum – but nobody has yet been able to pinpoint exactly what the issue is. Isabella's main problem is hoarding. She also checks and re-checks that the house is locked up before leaving it; this often makes her late.

She's talked of losing a necklace that was of great sentimental value to her mother, when she was a very little girl. Isabella had been told not to play with it, but used it when dressing up and somehow lost it. This obviously preyed on her mind as, when the family had their fitted carpet replaced some time later, she tried to check between the floorboards for the necklace, even though it was impossible for it to have fallen through the carpet. I have wondered whether this has somehow contributed to Isabella's hoarding. When she told me the story, I asked her about any possible link to her OCD, and it was apparent that this had never occurred to her. I do appreciate, however, that identifying any possible triggers doesn't necessarily help in "curing" someone of their OCD.

Isabella's ability to cope varies: my friend has made some efforts to clear out the stuff she has accumulated. Among other things, she keeps information in case she might need it: facts about clothes she might buy, or holidays she might go on. She feels guilty that her parents' home is being submerged by her stuff. She feels that they can't move on with their lives while she is still at home cluttering it up, but that isn't yet enough of a push for her to really tackle the problem head on. I try to encourage her by saying that any clearing out is better than nothing, and she should take one small step at a time. Isabella is also making efforts not to add to her existing hoard. She feels overwhelmed by the bigger picture and how far she still has to go. She is generally fearful of all of life's dangers and also feels guilty about how much of her life she has wasted on OCD activities. I repeatedly point out that it is better to look forward to how much of her life is still ahead and not to look back, but she finds it hard to do this.

Although Isabella and I only meet fortnightly, with occasional emails or chats in between, it can be quite challenging. Although I am further ahead in my own recovery from OCD, I am still an anxious person with some lingering habits. I understand where my friend is coming from, but I am not always sure of the best way to advise her as to how to get unstuck from her own position.

....

Types of Treatment for OCD

Fortunately, the old-fashioned view that people with OCD should pull themselves together and stop attention-seeking has been discounted. Within the past fifteen years plus, there has been huge progress in the effective treatment of OCD. No one knows yet exactly what causes OCD, but research is making headway as we speak.

Currently, the main theory for OCD is that abnormal levels of serotonin – a vital chemical messenger in the brain – are to blame. Serotonin is a neurotransmitter; nerve cells use it to communicate with one another. Serotonin acts in many biological processes,[1] including mood, aggression, impulse control, sleep, appetite, body temperature and pain. Serotonin dysregulation has also been implicated in depression, eating disorders, self-mutilation and schizophrenia (Yaryura-Tobias and Neziroglu, 1997).

COGNITIVE BEHAVIOURAL THERAPY (CBT)

Experts agree that Cognitive Behavioural Therapy (CBT) is a useful form of treatment. The "cognitive" in CBT refers to techniques that help to alter OCD faulty *beliefs*. "Behavioural" indicates specific methods for changing *actions,* such as the compulsive rituals, in OCD. Working with a trained CBT therapist, people with OCD learn that *they* are in charge, not the disorder.

Key cognitive errors in OCD sufferers are:[2]

- *Black and White Thinking:* If I don't do it perfectly, then I've done it wrongly.

- *Magical Thinking:* If I think a bad thought, it will certainly cause something horrible to happen.

- *Thought/Action Fusion*, which is similar to "Magical Thinking": If I have a bad thought about harming someone, it feels as though I've actually done it.

- *Overestimating Risk and Danger:* If I take even the slightest risk, something terrible is likely to happen.

- *Perfectionism* (self-explanatory).

- *Hyper-Morality:* I'll certainly go to hell, or be otherwise punished, for the slightest mistake.

- *Over-Responsibility for Others:* I must at all times guard against making a mistake that could possibly even remotely harm an innocent person.

- *Over-Importance of Thought:* If I think of a terrible event occurring, the likelihood of it actually happening is very high.

Other cognitive errors are:

- "What if?" thinking

- intolerance of uncertainty

- The Exclusivity Error – as in: "If something bad happens, it's more likely to happen to me, or to someone I love."

- The Nobility Gambit or Martyr Complex – as in: "How noble I am! I will gladly sacrifice my life doing endless rituals as a small price to pay to protect those I love."

What therapists say

> CBT is the best way of treating OCD there is, at
> this time. It depends on the client whether it's better
> to use it in conjunction with medication or not.
> **Irene Tubbs**

> CBT is an effective treatment for not very acute cases
> of OCD – when performing obsessions hasn't become
> a strong habit.
> **Rosie Thwaite**

> The CBT I practise has a lot of literature on the
> subject, but my learning is really enhanced through
> working with, and learning from, OCD clients.
> **Irene Tubbs**

> I act within the NICE guidelines, which
> recommend psychological intervention prior to
> introducing medication. All clinical evidence
> supports the efficacy of CBT.
> **Megan Karnes**

EXPOSURE AND RESPONSE PREVENTION (ERP)

ERP helps OCD sufferers realize that their fears don't come true and they can get used to – or "habituate" – the frightening feeling. For example, a teenager who repeatedly touches things in his room to prevent bad luck will learn to leave his room without touching anything.[3] He might be very scared initially – perhaps he'll feel worse before he starts to feel better – but after a while the anxiety departs as the teenager gets used to ERP. He learns that nothing bad happens. ERP repetition will cause the urges to lessen over time. Persistence and resistance are the keys as, at first, ERP might appear daunting to many OCD sufferers.

What therapists say

ERP is an essential part of treatment.

I do think exposure of the clients to their OCD fears is essential at some point. It must be done properly, with a gradual introduction and support from a therapist. There also needs to be family cognitive restructuring and understanding, with motivation from the client.
Dawn Cook

Typically, the person who has both physical rituals and intellectual ruminations is easier to engage, because they see evidence themselves from doing ERP.
Megan Karnes

Exposure of the patient to their fears is very useful.
Irene Tubbs

COUNSELLING/PSYCHOTHERAPY

People need to select their therapists as carefully as possible. If someone close to you with OCD is considering consulting one, the following information may be useful should you wish to help them find a suitable therapist.

Private therapy

If the person with OCD can afford it, they can choose to pay for therapy privately. The cost of talking therapy varies and currently a one-hour session can cost between £40 and £100. In the first instance, they should ask their GP if they can suggest a local private therapist.

Every therapist is different, as is every client, so what suits one person may not be right for another. A reputable therapist is a professional, being paid to carry out a service. Below is a list of questions to ask an OCD therapist before deciding whether they have the requisite skills to give treatment. The therapist should happily answer openly or in the affirmative to all these.

- Have you treated OCD before?

- How long have you been in practice treating OCD?

- How much does treatment cost?

- Will you set out a specific CBT treatment plan especially for your client?

- Will goals be set together?

- Do you use a technique called graded exposure?

- Do you set practical exercises or homework and help understanding in these exercises? (Where behavioural exercises are set for homework, a good proactive therapist will even come out to meet their client to do the exercises with them.)

- Do you provide cognitive and behavioural treatment, rather than just behavioural treatment?

- What is your position on medication? (If relevant for the person concerned.)

You or the person with OCD should talk to several therapists and also check their credentials and qualifications. There are no rules governing who can advertise talking therapy services, so it's essential to ensure that the therapist chosen is listed on one of the registers of approved practitioners. There are many official-sounding counselling and therapy bodies, but not all of them check the credentials of members.

OCD-UK recommends using therapists accredited with the British Association for Behavioural & Cognitive Psychotherapies (BABCP), the leading organization in the UK for CBT therapists. This is not to be confused with the British Association for Counselling & Psychotherapy (BACP). Again, although there are more than 7,500 members of BABCP, only about 1,500 are accredited.

The following organizations also have approved therapists; the same rules regarding checking them out apply:

- British Psychological Society: psychologists. (www.bps.org.uk/)

- British Association for Behavioural & Cognitive Psychotherapies (BABCP): cognitive behavioural therapists. (www.babcp.com/)

- Association for Family Therapy (AFT): family therapists. (www.aft.org.uk/)

- British Association for Counselling & Psychotherapy (BACP): counsellors and therapists. (www.bacp.co.uk/)

- UK Council for Psychotherapy (UKCP): psychotherapists. (www.psychotherapy.org.uk/)

Reasonably priced and free therapy

MIND charity
The charity MIND offers very reasonable or free talking therapies. (www.mind.org.uk/)

The NHS
It is government policy to make counselling and other talking treatments, including CBT, more easily available. The Improving Access to Psychological Therapies (IAPT) programme is currently rolling out until 2015. This is placing thousands more trained therapists in GP surgeries. A GP can refer someone for talking treatment that is free on the NHS. This will usually be a short course of counselling or CBT from the GP surgery's counselling service.

If counselling or CBT isn't available at the surgery, a GP can refer someone to a local counsellor or therapist for NHS treatment. Those requiring it may also be able to refer themselves for counselling. The IAPT programme means that increasingly primary care trusts (PCTs) are introducing the option of self-referral. Self-referral means that those who would prefer not to talk to their doctor can go directly to a professional therapist. Where possible, though, and unless there's a specific reason not to, it is better for people to discuss things with their GP first.

If you have access to a computer, you can find out what's available in your area by searching for psychological therapy services online.

EYE MOVEMENT DESENSITIZATION AND REPROCESSING (EMDR)

Although research into EMDR is in its infancy, it may prove useful for people with OCD. Clients hold in mind an image of a traumatic event in their lives, while simultaneously tracking the therapist's finger as it moves back and forth in front of their eyes. The combination of the mental activity and the external stimulus is believed to aid in reprocessing traumatic memories in ways that reduce their pain and damage to a person's life. This is a simple summary of a complicated procedure, but more details can be found at http://www.emdr.com/

ALTERNATIVE TREATMENTS

People with OCD are often suspicious of the traditional medical approach. However, while homeopathy, acupuncture, biofeedback and vitamin supplements, for example, may be useful in the treatment of various conditions, unfortunately their efficacy in OCD has yet to be proved.[4]

Whichever type of treatment is chosen – alternative or traditional – it's important to ensure that it's supported by legitimate research, plus proof that it works better than a placebo. Wrong treatment can be harmful.

A *therapist says*

> *To help people with OCD cope, I'd recommend*
> *normalizing such things as thinking, imagination,*
> *emotional purpose, stress-management techniques,*
> *CBT and REBT.*
> **Irene Tubbs**

Rational Emotive Behaviour Therapy (REBT) is a comprehensive psychotherapy that focuses on the resolving of emotional and behavioural problems.

MEDICATION

Clinical and scientific evidence has shown that CBT combined with medication is an effective treatment. It often helps those with OCD to enjoy happier lives.

Anti-depressants are usually the first type of medicine for OCD that a doctor will try. This medication may also be referred to as "Selective Serotonin-Reuptake Inhibitors" (SSRIs). These include:[5]

- fluvoxamine (Luvox®)

- fluoxetine (Prozac®)

- sertraline (Zoloft®)

- paroxetine (Paxil®)

- clomipramine (Anafranil®) – this is the oldest medication for OCD and is a tricyclic anti-depressant. Newer drugs that specifically target serotonin have been developed.

The following and other anti-depressants may also be of use, but more study is needed:

- citalopram (Celexa®)

- venlafaxine (Effexor)

- nafazodone (Serzone).

Side-effects may include:

- sleep problems

- restlessness

- weight fluctuation

- dry mouth

- nausea

- heartburn

- constipation

- diarrhoea

- dizziness

- sexual dysfunction

These drugs appear safe for long-term use, and side-effects reverse when they are stopped. There is no current evidence that they do permanent damage to the body.[6]

It is important to know that if the first medicine taken does not improve the OCD, another one should be tried. It may be necessary to try several types of OCD medicine. Many people have better results if CBT is added to drug treatment. If a drug and CBT don't work, combining more than one medicine may be attempted.[7]

Note: drinking alcohol is not a good idea when taking medication for OCD.

A therapist says

> Medication is wholly a choice. Clients' views of
> medication that involves the brain differ. For those
> who are able to accept that they have a disorder
> and they may need to take a daily pill to manage it,
> medication isn't an issue.
>
> Alternatively, the person who sees serotonin
> imbalance as a personal failure might think that
> psychiatric medications are "for them, not me". Such
> clients could see taking medication as failure to
> engage in treatment.
>
> This "I can beat it" mentality would be absurd
> regarding allergies, but is commonplace when
> dealing with issues of mental health.
>
> Often within the NHS, SSRIs are offered as
> the first mode of treatment. While it may work in
> some cases, it doesn't help the person challenge the
> emotional and psychological drivers.
>
> I consider medication without therapy to be
> unsuccessful: it can often make the person feel
> a failure.
>
> **Megan Karnes**

6

Other Treatments for OCD
....

HOSPITAL TREATMENT

What therapists say

> *Admittance to a psychiatric hospital and how*
> *helpful that might be for the person with OCD*
> *depends on them. Factors such as how old they are,*
> *how severe the condition, whether the patient is*
> *making a free choice or if they are being sectioned*
> *for their safety, or if the parent decides it is needed,*
> *come into play. Personally I think one-to-one*
> *treatment is best for the majority of OCD patients.*
> **Irene Tubbs**

> *For some patients, going to hospital for treatment for*
> *OCD can be very helpful.*
> *Most psychological out-patient services are*
> *located in, or are part of, a mental health service.*
> *Many of the people who are referred, are referred to*
> *a psychological unit.*
> *It is my understanding from clinical data*
> *that specialist OCD treatment can be beneficial*
> *in a hospital setting. I see no benefit in using in-*

patient treatment – detention under the Mental
Health Act – for those with OCD. This is because
the primary focus of admission is to stabilize the
individual via medication, instead of offering them
psychological support.
Megan Karnes

I would recommend a patient attend psychiatric
hospital if they were putting themselves or others in
danger, or can't function. It doesn't happen often.
In a few cases, hospitals help patients to deal with
OCD better long term.
Claire Hill

NEUROSURGERY

The majority of people with OCD will gain some relief from medication and CBT treatments, but there are a few who don't obtain adequate respite from their illness. Those who are very treatment-resistant are occasionally treated with neurosurgery. Usually the patient must have undergone intensive treatment for OCD for a minimum of five years beforehand (Jenike, 1998).

Neurosurgery does not always improve the symptoms of OCD. Importantly, though, treatments that didn't work prior to surgery might work well afterwards.[1]

(See Appendix A for more details regarding OCD and the brain.)

What a therapist says about their experience of OCD/treatment

OCD may be difficult to treat when the client
holds an amount of self-stigma combined with a
hierarchical view regarding mental health, such as
"us and them". This forms the strongest barrier to the

individual opting to take risks, such as challenging their beliefs.

My focus isn't the obliteration of intrusive thoughts and anxiety. I've worked effectively with a range of clients using a personalized intervention structure. This includes a cognitive and humanistic theoretical model. I want to enable people to find their own way, so I'm all in favour of them researching information themselves. Each person is an individual: as such they progress according to their own tolerance and ability.

OCD is a disorder that feeds on itself. Personal isolation only fuels it. As OCD moves into an increasingly stronger position, it can be more difficult for the person to see it as separate. If something is telling you – not as psychosis – that you need to do something for safety, it takes a very strong individual to then take the risk not to carry out an OCD ritual.
Megan Karnes

TREATMENTS TO AVOID[2]

Systematic desensitization
This treatment involves relaxation in association with feared images and objects. It is not advisable for "contamination" OCD, as many people find they cannot engage in relaxation exercises when they are "in the moment" of contamination fears. If this portion fails, then the whole treatment falls apart and the only thing left is frustration.

Cognitive disputations
Many people feel that directly challenging "faulty beliefs" associated with OCD is demeaning, as it can result in an ongoing argument with the treatment provider. Cognitive

therapy is widely used for "contamination" OCD, but proper use involves a style that is entirely tailored to the case concerned.

Analysis

Some professionals still believe that OCD is best treated through lengthy analysis. There is a strong argument that this fails in two ways. First, symptoms can continue for a long time with no relief in sight. Secondly and more seriously, analysis can foster doubt. As people with OCD already suffer from this, it can make symptoms worse.

Thought-stopping

This approach takes the form of the person with OCD keeping a rubber band on their wrist and every time the urge arises to unnecessarily wash, for example, they snap the rubber band against the skin. The goal is for the person to be able to remove the rubber band and instead say "Stop" to themselves, as a means of preventing ritual washing.

This actually creates a worsening of symptoms. There is plenty of research showing that this is a harmful way of proceeding for any clients with mental health problems.

....

Interview: Patricia Church, therapist

I've been in practice treating OCD, among other conditions, for seventeen years now. Originally, I decided to work with people with OCD because they presented with this issue in its various forms and I wanted to help.

Most of my work is private, rather than NHS-based, with mainly British clients. The majority of them find me via the BACP website. Currently, 25 per cent of my clients have OCD. Interestingly, I would have answered 5 to 10 per cent instead, which is my usual experience, before I checked the figures. Only four of my patients have been aged under sixteen in the last two years, but this is an increase on five years ago. Most of the OCD sufferers I treat are men, and on average they've had OCD since childhood – for ten to twenty years. OCD is linked to depression in half of the cases I see.

I didn't find it difficult getting information about OCD seventeen years ago when I first began treating the illness. Nowadays, I look online, read books and attend courses on it to keep abreast of the latest developments. I don't find OCD difficult to diagnose, and it's not a problem for me if clients have trawled the Internet for information before they arrive. OCD is difficult to treat, though, particularly in older, longstanding clients. When they've complied with the illness's demands over a long period, it becomes progressive and more entrenched. The patient finds it harder to alter their patterns of behaviour. Younger clients are much easier to help. Incidentally, in my experience, young people take great pains to hide their condition. I expect schools and other educational institutions would be supportive if they were aware of what was happening.

The number of OCD clients seems to have risen during the past five years, due to growing public awareness. There's also a general acceptance now of counselling, without feelings of shame being attached to it. However, there isn't enough public knowledge about OCD – there is little understanding of intrusive thoughts. I would recommend that people in close contact with an OCD sufferer should combat the illness by never playing along with it. Use counselling support too, and read about the condition. OCD is more understood in our society than in the past, but is still too often treated and publicized only as a titillating interest. I would say that people with severe OCD are officially "disabled".

I've often been impressed by family support for clients, but largely disappointed by their lack of understanding of how to aid the person with OCD. With regard to traumatic life events perhaps triggering OCD – I have seen at least three teenage boys developing the condition after an illness or accident befalling their fathers. I think they experience life as scary and out of their control, so they try lucky or magic rituals. Clients often perform rituals. They will do a task a certain number of times, such as safety-checking, or saying goodbye many times.

About 70 to 80 per cent of the individuals I see worry about issues, instead of performing rituals. They often fear that they will cause harm to others or that they are bad people. On a positive note, I've rarely come across discrimination against or the bullying of a patient.

To help OCD sufferers cope, I would recommend that they remind themselves that it is a medical condition. It's the brain sending false messages. Remember: "It's not me, it's my OCD." Others can support sufferers in their struggle not to act on these communications. To help carers cope, I would say don't play along with thoughts or rituals; also inform yourself about OCD.

Cognitive Behavioural Therapy can play a very big part in treatment. In my view, anti-anxiety medication together with CBT interventions in a person-centred therapy is the best way forward. (GPs, knowing the patient's history, would always make the decision as to the best medication.) At some stage, exposure of the client to their fears, increasing slowly, has to be undertaken in order to make progress in treatment. Another OCD treatment, rationalizing, can play a part, with praise for success. A particularly unsuccessful treatment would be trying to force thoughts to go away. If I perceive the condition to be chronic and completely taking over the client's life, then I'd recommend that they attend a psychiatric hospital. I've only ever experienced a client in this state once, though.

PUBLIC ACCESS TO TREATMENT

What therapists say

I don't think the public can access professional treatment for OCD easily enough. It's a treatable disorder, but people aren't getting the support.
Megan Karnes

The NHS only looks at the cost of treatment and does not take into account the overall cost of not intervening. Therapy given, as initially stated by the NICE guidelines, costs money and time. No consideration is given to the fact that therapy not being given can take an individual from work to benefits.
Megan Karnes

There's no accounting for how much value is lost when bright people are felled by OCD. It wouldn't be acceptable in any other context.
Megan Karnes

Professional treatment for OCD is not accessible enough. Family members are extremely frustrated with the NHS – particularly concerning transition from child to adult services. At least provision on the NHS for cheap or free treatment has improved since IAPT, and the huge increase in the number of therapists. Long waiting lists still occur in secondary care, though.
Beryl Jackson

NHS waiting times are eight to twelve months. If people with OCD can't afford private treatment, they're forced to suffer.
Patricia Church

Interview: Claire Hill, therapist

People think they know what OCD is, but they certainly don't have a full understanding of its impact. It's quite a common disorder: lots of the people who come to see me have OCD, but sometimes they're unaware of it. The majority of my clients are referred to me from school, and/or come for treatment privately. I've currently got 301 clients with OCD (equally split between the sexes) and 50 per cent of them are aged under sixteen. Clients usually carry out rituals, and mine also obsessively worry about issues.

Sometimes OCD can be difficult to treat – it depends on how severe it is and if the patient is prepared to change. By the time I meet adult clients, they've usually had OCD for ten years or more. I think it's related to the type of OCD behaviour they have, whether clients find it harder to change the way they live. It has not been my experience that it's normal for trauma to have happened around the time of onset of the condition.

There's a lot of anxiety-provoking nonsense in cyber-space: it can make my job harder if people have looked up info about OCD on the Internet before I see them. Most of the time OCD is easy to identify, even though it can be linked to other conditions. The public are more knowledgable about OCD now, but it would be good to have accurate information more freely available. The majority of my clients have experienced stigma concerning mental illness. On the upside, though, the schools my younger clients attend have a good understanding of students with OCD.

If carers are able to support those they know with OCD in changing their patterns of behaviour, it can be a win-win situation. I don't consider patients with this condition to be officially disabled, but coping with daily life can be very difficult for them. Support groups are very helpful, but I couldn't set one up – no time. The situation in general would also be improved by professional treatment for OCD being more easily accessible.

Cognitive Behavioural Therapy works for some sufferers, but I've found there are other issues as well and long-term therapy functions better then. What is particularly unsuccessful treatment-wise is sufferers being given only three sessions with a therapist, by medical cover.

....

7

Advice for Parents of Children and Teenagers / Students with OCD

Useful tips from parents of children with OCD

- Life does get better. And sometimes it will get better and then worse – but it will get better again. You just have to keep working and trying. OCD can be managed and the sufferer can have a fantastic life. And if you need medication to get to that point, it's OK; just be mindful and informed. OCD is nobody's fault: it is a brain disorder.

- We got Lucy to draw her OCD and she drew this blue circular being with thin arms and legs. I knitted one for her, a soft toy, and "Germy", as she named it, often gets punched, squashed and thrown across the room.

- I wish someone had said to me early on: "It's not your fault; you didn't cause this. You are not a bad parent." Even after I was assured of these things, it took me time to believe them.

- Read about the disorder from reputable sources; try to empower yourself so as to help your loved one.

- *Always be positive and unconditional in your support for the OCD sufferer. Remind them, when you are challenging certain behaviours, that you are helping them fight back against the OCD, rather than just saying no to them.*

- *Keep a sense of humour and try to stay positive. Difficult, though, as it blights my son's life! I so wish I'd known earlier that my son is not alone.*

- *Start remedial work for the person concerned as soon as possible, with a well-qualified person in the subject. Easier said than done, though!*

- *Seek help, contact a self-help group, discuss it.*

- *OCD uses up the energy of everyone involved. Get therapy yourself if possible, so that you have a supportive place to explore your own experience.*

- *Build the muscle of living with the other person's anxiety – you can then help them to develop that emotional and psychological muscle. This will give you both strength to stand up to the OCD bully.*

- *Exercise helps keep me sane. Find appropriate help for someone with OCD as soon as possible. Be sure that the sufferer engages well with the therapist.*

- *Tell other people about the situation and encourage the sufferer to do so as well – that way everyone feels less isolated.*

- *Exercise has been extremely helpful for me and my daughter. It helps tire her out and calm her thoughts – the same for me. It also gives me an escape.*

- *Educate yourself. The more you learn, the more you will realize that you are not alone. There is so much good help available out there, you will find the key to successfully living with OCD.*

DIAGNOSIS

If you think your young child might have OCD, the first thing to do is to speak with their GP. With older children or teenagers, they may prefer to speak to the GP alone, but you should encourage them to seek help.

To aid assessment, there is also a children's version of the Yale-Brown Obsessive–Compulsive Scale (YBOCS) questionnaire.

Child and Adolescent Mental Health (CAMH) run a website for professionals, young people and parents. (http://www.camh.org.uk/)

Useful website
http://school.ocdaction.org.uk/parents/

EDUCATING GPS

Unfortunately, some doctors still have little knowledge of OCD. If this is your experience, OCD-UK has an icebreaker, which can be printed off from their website (http://www.ocduk.org/ice-breaker) or requested by post. The icebreaker explains what OCD is. Also, it indicates that you know your child needs to be diagnosed and offered CBT treatment.

Your GP may then arrange a referral to your local Child and Adolescent Mental Health Services (CAMHS). Here, you and/or your child will be able to discuss the symptoms with a mental health professional. They will have the expertise to diagnose and treat the OCD.

FAMILY DYNAMICS

There's no doubt that OCD – as with any mental health problem – can hit families very hard, often with a sort of ripple effect. This anxiety disorder needs to be recognized and professionally treated as soon as possible, particularly in children. OCD must not be ignored, mocked or minimized – it does not make the illness go away, and causes additional distress to the sufferer.

Below are some responses to OCD by relatives:

- *When he was five, my brother used to do a little jump when we were in the street, then hit his head with his hands or licked his fingers. My mum didn't understand and used to get cross. She told James he'd go blind if he licked his fingers. Mum had to do a lot of cleaning but she wouldn't get a new carpet, even though James spoilt the other one by spitting. I remember when he had OCD so badly – he was eleven – that he couldn't leave his room. He used to go to the loo in bottles, but then he couldn't throw them away. My mum has read stuff about OCD and she understands much better now.*

- *My sister has had serious mental health issues, but tries to lay down the law about how I should treat my daughter who has OCD.*

- *I sometimes have to ask her brother to do something, or forgive something of Lucy. It isn't always totally reasonable and he gets understandably annoyed.*

- *Other family members know about the OCD and accommodate my daughter if necessary. Lots of people have little OCD tendencies and I think it has made us all examine our own idiosyncrasies.*

What therapists say

Relatives often undermine sufferers' fears, viewing them as something which could be controlled by willpower, because they don't have enough information. If that can be put straight, I've found families are usually very supportive.
Rosie Thwaite

I attempt to empower OCD carers with information on what works and what doesn't. Often people just see the different types of OCD behaviour without understanding the cause.
Megan Karnes

I've lost count of the number of times I've told a relative that although they think they're doing the right thing by giving in to the OCD bully, they are actually feeding the monster.
Megan Karnes

It is hell to stand up to OCD. However, a person who cares for a child wouldn't let that child eat chocolate as a staple diet. Likewise, a person who cares about the person with OCD has to refuse to acquiesce to rituals as a short-term fix.
Megan Karnes

Relatives and friends of OCD sufferers need to understand the condition and, importantly, how OCD is maintained.
Ruby Moore

Carers should meet the therapist so that they understand how to support the patient. I've worked with many parents of adolescents with OCD. To support the youngsters, the parents need to understand both OCD and the rationale for treatment, for example CBT.

They then need to support the patient with OCD; for example, help them achieve long-term goals and aid them with between-session work.
Ruby Moore

HOW TO TREAT OCD IN CHILDREN AND TEENAGERS

Cognitive Behavioural Therapy (CBT)

Experts agree that Cognitive Behavioural Therapy (CBT) is the treatment of choice for children and adolescents with OCD. Working with a trained CBT therapist, young people with OCD learn that *they* are in charge, not the disorder.

During CBT, the child or adolescent is encouraged to identify inaccurate thoughts and replace them with healthier ones.

Exposure and Response Prevention (ERP)

The CBT technique considered most effective in the treatment of OCD is Exposure and Ritual Prevention (ERP),[1] also known as Exposure and Response Prevention. Using this, individuals can learn to combat OCD by facing their fears gradually in small steps (exposure), without capitulating to the rituals (response prevention).

At first, ERP might appear daunting to many OCD sufferers, particularly children and adolescents. Persistence and resistance are the keys.[2]

Psychotherapy

Therapists need to be chosen as carefully as possible. Obviously for a child, the person needs to have a child-friendly practice and plenty of experience of treating the particular age group concerned. It is also important to take time to verify the therapist's credentials and qualifications. There are many official-sounding counselling and therapy bodies, but not all of them check the credentials of their members. (See Chapter 5 for a list of suggested questions to ask when choosing a therapist.)

Medication

Both CBT and medication can be used to effectively treat children and adolescents. Different types of medicine should only be considered, though, when a young patient has moderate to severe OCD symptoms. OCD medicine controls and decreases symptoms, but does not "cure" the disorder. Symptoms often return when the child stops taking the medicine.

Only four OCD medicines have been approved by the FDA for use in children[3] –Prozac, Luvox, Anafranil and Zoloft – but doctors can prescribe any type of OCD medicine for children if they think it's necessary. (Anafranil is not usually prescribed first, because of its side-effects.) Something to bear in mind is that all OCD medication works slowly. It is important not to give up on the medicine until it has been taken at the right dose for ten to twelve weeks.[4] Studies have also shown that improvement of childhood OCD can continue for at least a year after the start of medication. The best dose of OCD medicine should be determined on an individual basis. Children should start at a lower dose than adolescents, but OCD symptoms often require the use of higher, adult-sized doses.[5] If the child has difficulty swallowing pills, a liquid or other version may be available.

A child's response to each of the OCD medicines varies – no two children respond in the same way. Factors that may guide the medicine choice include:

• positive response to a certain drug by other family members

• the presence of other disorders

• potential for side-effects

• cost or availability.

In a child OCD treatment study, remission occurred in about one in five children on medicine, and in more than half of those being treated with medicine and CBT. Many more children also improved, though not to the extent of full remission. (If patients don't respond at all, this does not mean that other medicine won't help.)

Every type of drug has potential side-effects, which must always be weighed against its benefits. For all anti-depressants given to children and adolescents, the FDA has issued "black box warnings" about associated suicidal thoughts and urges. The highest risk period for this is when starting or increasing the dose of the medicine. However, a recent study found no increase in suicidal thoughts or behaviour from paediatric OCD groups studied.

Feedback from parent

Audrey's daughter stopped taking medication after turning eighteen:

Sarah's adolescent care was brilliant. She had two psychiatrists: one male, one female. They were both fantastic and she trusted them. The family therapy side was very good then. However, in the past two years – since she turned eighteen – after being discharged from the Mental Health Unit, Sarah decided not to take her medication. Her father and I weren't allowed input to the psychologist now without her permission. She refused to give it. It led to a terrible six months. She failed her exams at the end of the course she was on (despite being awarded a merit the year before). She became aggressive and paranoid. She sent us abusive texts; she hit me. I showed the bruises to her psychologist; she didn't want to listen, though, as I wasn't the patient. In desperation I went to our GP, asking for help. The GP called a care meeting and now, two years on, they listen to us.

When OCD is very severe, it is sometimes recommended that children are given medication normally reserved for older people.

Interview: Sheila and Angus

Sheila: *Angus and I didn't want Lucy to have drugs at such a young age. She was just ten. But there didn't seem to be any choice. The medication isn't licensed for under-twelves, so that gives an idea of how bad the OCD was. The medication made a difference, but Lucy still goes through very bad periods with the illness. It has never gone away. She's now had CBT and Eye Movement Desensitization and Reprocessing (EMDR), plus she is on sertraline. It has gone up to 100 mg/day, but her OCD is pretty bad at the moment so it might need to be increased again. This is the only medicine she's been prescribed, but presumably at her age there is not the same choice as for an adult.*

Angus: *She's had a fair bit of CBT, too. We had one lot with a private psychologist, then when Lucy took a turn for the worse and needed medication, we transferred to CAMHS. She had some more there.*

Sheila: *It helped and it didn't help. We dealt with some of her contamination fears. Lucy found it hard, but we had a reward chart to encourage her and she made some progress before the OCD took a turn for the worse. We still don't know what triggered that. She suddenly went downhill quickly and was barely functioning. It was very frightening. The EDMR seemed to work well, though: Lucy has done quite a few sessions, where particular issues or memories were worked on. All the psychologists and psychiatrists were very good and knowledgeable about OCD – the same with CBT.*

I'd recommend a Worry-Busters group that Lucy attended, along with five other children. It looked at coping strategies, and the group leaders gave out separate info for parents. From my point of view, I liked having the opportunity to speak to other parents who knew what I was talking about. Lucy liked the group as it was the first time she had met other children with similar issues (none with OCD, but there were some similarities). The problem with strategies, though, is that an OCD thing can come out of the blue. Lucy can't calm down sufficiently to think: "Oh yes, I should try deep breathing."

Our old GP was amazing... he suffered from OCD as well and told me that, aged eleven, he had to take a year out of school as he was so ill with it. He was brilliant, so supportive, and always asked after Lucy whenever I saw him. Unfortunately he retired and the GP I have now doesn't seem to understand it at all. He wanted Lucy to come off the medication, without asking the psychiatrist. He also says things that are very ignorant and occasionally upsetting.

Lucy was traumatized by events two years ago, when she was nine. In an eighteen-month period she was admitted to hospital as an emergency four times. Just before the OCD started, she developed appendicitis when I was camping with her and her brother. She was taken by ambulance to the nearest hospital and we were miles away from home. She thought she was going to die – the pain was horrific.

People casually mention OCD without any concept of what it's really like. It's not just washing your hands a bit much, although initially Lucy did that. I noticed her hands were red and cracked. After a visit to the psychiatrist, Lucy was sobbing and couldn't stop. I had to lift her bodily from the clinic to the car, which was parked in a supermarket car park. One positive thing came out of that day – well, two, if you count the psychiatrist ringing up to check we were OK. She said she had a rule that she never rang clients at home, but had been worried by hearing Lucy crying outside all the way to the car park. The silver lining was that Lucy was catatonic in the psychiatrist's office, so the psychiatrist saw it. I think she called it "dissociation from reality". She said that normally patients behaving like this were hospitalized and given drugs.

Lucy copes better during the school holidays than in term-time, but luckily she generally holds it together at school. She's intelligent and good at the work, which is a valuable morale booster for her. There have still been episodes at school, but the teachers are aware of her OCD. Most of her rituals happen at bedtime. Sometimes they change or vary slightly. Lucy has a certain ritual for going to the toilet, using particular hands to do particular things. She will not pull her trousers up until she has washed her hands. When her OCD was particularly bad, she removed all her clothes before going to the toilet. As Lucy's major fear is contamination, toilets are one of the worst things she has to cope with. She also counts things, and taps objects a certain number of times.

Angus: *Lucy's main anxieties are to do with germs, so she constantly worries about what she's touched, whether it has contaminated her, etc. At one time she was very concerned about germs and the cat, as they wash in their own spit and are therefore "dirty". She refused to stroke the cat and wouldn't sit down in the house apart from on one cushion, as she didn't know what the cat had touched. She worries about PE lessons held outside, as another major fear is contamination from foliage of any kind.*

Sheila: *Lucy worries if she's watching a TV programme and thinks she didn't hear something properly. She will sit and rewind the programme numerous times if necessary. She also worries if she doesn't think she's said something in the right way. She gets stressed sometimes when she's reading, as she feels as though she has to remember all the words on the page.*

Angus: *What is interesting now is that when the OCD gets really bad, Lucy's body breaks down. We had to take her to A&E not long ago with terrible hip pain. Before that it was with a bad knee. Lucy has also been deaf – but only temporarily.*

Sheila: *One of the reasons the idea of your book interested me is because I couldn't find a book specifically aimed to be helpful to me. When OCD was diagnosed, I thought, "I can't be the only mother of a nine-year-old with this," but I couldn't find much aimed at the parents. I did my own research, as there weren't any leaflets in the GP's surgery. The only problem with doing that is that you can scare yourself on the Internet. The first psychologist we saw gave me a leaflet that she had put together, formed of tips from other parents.*

Angus: *Our relationship with Lucy has altered.*

Sheila: *Yes, we are constantly aware of things that we know will upset her. As her mother, I feel I have to provide constant reassurance but try not to become part of her rituals. I feel I have to protect her, anticipate problems and think up coping strategies. Lucy doesn't want to do the same as her peers, such as sleepovers, in case that person has pets. I make excuses for her that don't invite questions, because she doesn't want her friends to know. I also have to explain to teachers why Lucy needs a special eye on her in certain situations. The teachers at school are aware of the situation and try to be supportive. I can't get cross with Lucy, as her anxiety means she can't cope with it. I can't ask her to make decisions – even about what chocolate she would like – because she worries about making the wrong choice. Our relationship seems to be different to the relationships I see between her peers and their mothers. I'm sure there's much more, but basically it boils down to feeling a lot more protective. I suppose I feel like a carer sometimes and not a mother.*

I desperately wanted to find a support group and looked high and low, without any luck. All I wanted to do was talk about it, but there was nowhere to go. That sounds a bit "me, me, me", but at the beginning when it was all so new, I didn't know which way to turn. I was very emotional and I needed an outlet for it, so that I stayed strong for Lucy. I don't have the confidence to set up a support group, but if a group was set up locally, I would do everything I could to help get it off the ground and running smoothly.

Angus: *At least our relationship with friends and relatives hasn't really altered. Other family members know about the OCD and accommodate her if necessary. Sheila and I were only talking today about the fact that luckily, a few years ago, we bought a fake Christmas tree, as Lucy now has a fear of any kind of foliage. Having said that, holidays are fine – we go skiing and she doesn't mind being outside in the snow, or falling over in it. I think that all the whiteness somehow seems "pure" to her. Equally, Lucy is fine when we go on holiday to Portugal; she seems happy to be on the sand or in the sea.*

Sheila: *Lucy was only nine when it started. Usually at that age any health problems are short-term, sorted out with a bit of Calpol. At the beginning I kept thinking we would find the magic answer – that somehow it would all be OK in the end. I do wish someone had told us early on to prepare for the worst. That there were no quick fixes and not necessarily a cure. It's a long-term thing and chirpily being told that it will be sorted in six weeks – which is what the paediatric consultant told me at the first appointment – wasn't very helpful. It gave us false hope.*

I think that the general public's perception of OCD is vastly different from the reality. I have found people are supportive, but they don't really "get it". Lucy became very upset at school recently because she thought that her blazer had been contaminated in a science lesson. A well-meaning female teacher took her to one side and Lucy spoke about the OCD. The teacher, obviously trying to make her feel better, said: "Oh, I completely understand. I'm OCD about my lounge curtains." That confused Lucy.

She had to put up with a bit of teasing at primary school because of the excessive hand-washing, but in general the kids just knew that Lucy was a bit different and accepted her. She has a good sense of humour and makes people laugh, which has helped a lot with friendships. At secondary school there is the odd comment, but Lucy refuses to be drawn on it; she keeps quiet. She has a close group of friends.

Eating regularly is important: if Lucy is hungry, she copes less well. She refuses to eat any fruit or vegetables, so that's tricky. As parents we stick to a healthy diet, which helps with energy levels.

Lucy does Taekwondo twice a week. She used to do tap and ballet dancing and go swimming, but those activities fell by the wayside – more casualties of OCD. She could barely get through the day at one point, never mind dance or swim. I think it must be good for her, getting the endorphins pumping, though I've not really thought about whether it helps the OCD. When I exercise, I actively enjoy the release of stress. I notice more and more that my brain just needs that space.

....

Interview: Betty's daughter

Alice's OCD was diagnosed a year ago, when she was seven years old. She is currently on medication.

Prior to treatment, my daughter Alice would obsessively fasten and unfasten her shoes. She would insist that I do it as well. I had to do it at least three times, or she would fly into a violent rage. She would also roll up the sleeves of both her dress and jacket until they were three inches above her wrist. Nothing could touch her wrists and Alice would continually check her sleeves throughout the day, to ensure that they were far enough away from that area.

At first I mistook Alice's symptoms as signs of some kind of sensory disorder. She was preoccupied with her clothing and would have frequent, intense meltdowns regarding how her clothes felt. She was constantly adjusting her outfit and complaining that nothing felt right. At various times Alice would accuse me of shrinking her clothing or secretly replacing it with articles that were too large. She went as far as to hide things from me and wear exactly the same outfit day after day, not allowing me to wash it.

I took her to our family doctor, expecting to be referred on for some short-term occupational therapy. Instead the doctor explained that my daughter clearly had OCD. I was stunned and disbelieving. Despite my misgivings, I immediately took my daughter to see an expert in childhood anxiety disorders, who confirmed our doctor's diagnosis after several visits. After nine months of weekly cognitive therapy, we decided to add Zoloft to our treatment regimen for Alice. Being only seven, she was having difficulty implementing some of the cognitive coping tools she was being taught. The decision to medicate my daughter was very painful and not one made lightly. I spent several tearful solo sessions talking with her therapist as I came to terms with the necessity of it.

Zoloft is the first medication we've tried because it worked well for me when I was suffering from depression. The doctor thought it was a good place to start, considering that my daughter is genetically similar to me. It made a tremendous difference in my daughter's compulsion to carry out rituals. Also, it helped alleviate the intrusive and obsessive thoughts she was suffering from.

My daughter currently takes 75 mg of Zoloft. We continue weekly therapy, as the medication isn't a magical cure-all. Alice still needs to learn how to cope with her issues. She has difficulty managing unstructured time or unexpected events, which leads to the occasional meltdown. Alice is now able to dress and function normally otherwise, which is a tremendous relief for the whole family.

My husband and I had to learn to adjust our parenting, as we could not expect our daughter to respond normally to traditional methods of discipline. Learning how to respond productively to her issues helped immensely. She wasn't being stubborn or obstinate; she honestly couldn't respond to our expectations properly. Alice was abnormally obsessed with watching television at one point: she had rituals regarding this activity and was desperate to watch it constantly. She would ask me repeatedly when she could watch a show, even if I had just answered her.

When my daughter started having issues I was confused, scared, and often frustrated and angry. At times I was convinced she was purposely antagonizing me with unreasonable behaviour. Alice refused to listen to "reason" – she was very inflexible and rigid in her thinking. Learning that this inflexibility is a symptom of my daughter's OCD allowed me to let go of my anger and frustration. There is nothing personally directed at me in terms of her behaviour. She has a disorder; it's out of her control. At times I still feel frightened and confused by her actions, but now I do not take these or her words personally, I am much calmer. I'm able to focus on responding to her needs.

Shortly before the onset of Alice's OCD last year, we moved from Columbus, Ohio, to Seattle, Washington. A few weeks later, Alice started kindergarten. It was the combination of these two major events that is thought to have brought on her condition. We were living in a small apartment in Seattle when her symptoms first occurred. We've now moved a couple of miles to a family home, in hopes that a more normal environment will ease some of my daughter's symptoms.

At times I feel isolated from other parents with "normal" children. My daughter is well liked by her peers, and functions perfectly in the structured environment of school, so people are often surprised and sometimes suspicious when it's revealed that she has OCD. She looks "normal" and she's not displaying obsessive–compulsive behaviour in public, so I feel like I have to defend her diagnosis. At times I feel like I am being treated like one of those parents who are overly quick to medicate their children and pursue a diagnosis to justify their bad parenting.

Alice currently attends weekly CBT appointments. In the beginning we saw the therapist twice weekly, as our family was in crisis. It has helped immensely. Through therapy alone, we were able to ease the worst of the obsessive–compulsive behaviour, especially regarding clothing and shoes. It was very hard work for my daughter but she was determined. The therapist challenged Alice to put on a different dress each day and wear it for five minutes, at the end of which she would get a reward. My daughter responded and soon enough she was trying on dresses and then totally forgetting her anxiety.

My mother is especially concerned about Alice, and spends far too much time reading worrying things on the Internet. I often get concerned calls from her fretting about her granddaughter's future; I have to reassure her that Alice is poised to have a perfectly normal, successful life. I try to stay off the Internet, frankly, as the information can be contradictory, alarming, or plainly wrong. I look to the professionals involved in my daughter's treatment for guidance. I'm lucky in that our extended family and close friends have been wonderful. For people outside of that circle, I find myself explaining, justifying, and defending the issue. It's just not common, and people are either curious or disbelieving. It can be exhausting.

I had to rely on my family doctor and our therapist to help me understand how OCD affects Alice, and what it means for her future. She was so young at the onset of her condition that it was difficult to find relevant information about OCD. Most of it was geared towards teenagers or adults, and I've noticed the symptoms in those groups can differ significantly from those that present in young children. I don't currently attend an OCD support group, as they are geared towards teenagers or adults. I have touched base with a few parents of young children suffering from OCD, but frankly it seems uncommon prior to adolescence. It's really helpful talking to other parents who are experiencing what we go through. Our family doctor is extremely helpful.

She consults regularly with a child psychiatrist regarding my daughter's medication.

When my daughter was first diagnosed, I met with the school staff. They were stunned to hear of her diagnosis since she wasn't disruptive at school. While they wanted to help her succeed, no one was sure what to do. It was up to me to come up with ideas, which was quite intimidating as I was rather confused myself. Her classmates know that she has frequent doctor appointments (therapy and medication adjustments) but don't really think much of it. The structure and routine of school is very soothing to her, so she thrives there. This school is one of the highest ranked elementary schools in the States, and relatively small. I believe this certainly makes a difference. Teachers are very understanding in terms of my daughter needing to make her appointments, but otherwise we are on our own. That's currently acceptable as my daughter feels safe and in control at school. When we make the move to middle school and high school, it may change. Alice is extremely concerned about public embarrassment. While she did used to compulsively pick at her clothing at school, she otherwise had few public symptoms. She would have pent-up anxiety and frustration which she would release the moment I picked her up at the end of the school day. This meant I had a sobbing, screaming, flailing heap of a child to try to drag home.

I've found that a great deal of sugar will trigger a meltdown, but otherwise we have not made dietary changes since Alice's diagnosis. Our diet is already well thought out as we do not eat gluten – my husband is gluten intolerant – or foods containing high fructose corn syrup. Cutting out high fructose corn syrup eliminated most processed foods. Also, all of our meat and dairy products are certified organic.

We find exercise useful: my daughter requires structured activity and lots of time in the playground. We try to play there for an hour after school each day. For me, exercise puts me in a better frame of mind, and it's important time for myself.

Holidays continue to be challenging. The deviation from the normal family routine triggers my daughter's anxiety. We try to schedule many activities and have a calendar she can reference. Alice does not cope well with free time. It can be exhausting when all you want to do is sit around and spend some time together. It's hard to find the right balance that works for us all. Attempts to help my daughter calm herself during a meltdown have been relatively futile. She is simply too far gone and completely out of control when it happens.

We turned to music lessons, as we were told that people with OCD typically do quite well with music. There is some correlation to the need for structure, I think. Anyway, we discovered that my daughter is musically gifted; playing and composing music has proved to be a rewarding and soothing activity for her. My child doesn't want to have meltdowns. She doesn't want to have intrusive thoughts or obsess about tying her shoes. It makes her unhappy. She isn't doing it to "get" to me or exert control over the household.

....

COPING TIPS

Sometimes those with OCD find it difficult to enter and leave rooms. One teenager was resourceful and would gently shunt her terrier across her bedroom threshold, to enable her to feel confident enough to follow suit. Her family caught on to this and, to see their daughter at meals, would furtively push the bewildered dog into her room. They would then whistle the animal out again and rush downstairs with it to the dinner table.

It can be very expensive, not to mention wasteful, if youngsters suddenly refuse to eat certain food, or wear particular items of clothing. There has been good feedback about the helpfulness of staff in clothes shops if OCD problems are explained. For example, Paula, ten years old, could not bear to read or hear people say "pregnant". She was obsessed with the dire imagined repercussions she associated with this word. Everything was adversely affected if "pregnant" cropped up. The family had arrived at a long-planned holiday destination. At last they were walking to the beach, much to her mother Sophie's relief. It had been difficult to arrange the break, due to Paula's OCD fears and obsessions. It had taken almost a day just for Paula to choose her new swimming costume at a shop. Paula, carefully carrying the new costume rolled in a towel, passed two Scandinavian tourists: "I think you mean pregnant?" one of them said loudly to the other. Paula dropped her towel as if it was radioactive. She backed away along the pavement and refused to go near the crumpled swimming costume lying on the ground. Her mother quickly decided to try to change the costume for a new one at a local branch of the store. She sent the family on ahead to the beach. At the shop, there were no costumes in her daughter's size left. In desperation, the mother asked the assistant at the till if she could put a new tag on the original garment so that it would appear newly bought. The assistant was very helpful when Sophie explained about the OCD. The costume was duly tagged and peace was restored.

Books for children aged five to twelve with OCD/anxiety issues
http://www.worrybusters.com/dig.htm

Children's books featuring OCD
http://www.amazon.com/Mr-Worry-Story-about-OCD/
dp/0807551821

EDUCATING SCHOOLS

The decision as to whether or not to inform your child's school of the OCD situation will depend on your own and your child's preferences.[6] It will also depend on the severity of the

OCD. Some schools know of it, but don't fully understand the disorder: "Oh yes, washing hands too often."

Teachers and friends may already be aware of a child's OCD if the pupil is very young, as there's often little attempt to hide the symptoms at that age. However, older children and adolescents may be better able, and under more pressure, to conceal their illness from teaching staff and peers. The student could be having problems completing homework because of OCD. They could also feel isolated, due to difficulty in maintaining social relationships. Your son or daughter may also be under huge stress due to OCD and exams. Informing the school of the student's OCD could be a beneficial and supportive move, but the child must feel involved in the decision. It might also be useful to provide the school with information on OCD. The OCD-UK website provides a section for teachers and other staff at the back of their information guide for parents.
http://www.ocduk.org/ocd-information-guide

(Other useful website addresses can be found at the end of this book.)

Feedback from parent

> *I don't think either of my daughter's schools had had to deal with OCD before. Her primary school was excellent. The teacher spoke to the psychologist about strategies for our daughter, and she had designated teachers to go to if she had a problem. The office staff knew and everybody dealt with it very well. Secondary school is different; you can't have that sort of attention. The teachers know about the OCD, and if I anticipate a problem I contact them to warn them. When she has had an episode at school they ring to let me know. I can't fault either of the schools: members of staff have been well-meaning and supportive.*

HELPING A TEENAGED STUDENT

Managing aspects of daily life in a healthy way can reduce stress, despite the presence of OCD. It is particularly easy in the first flush of student life to drop, or want to jettison, healthy habits – which ultimately aids the condition. The intrusion of OCD can easily lead to the neglect of personal care and interest, due to its "demeaning" nature. Here are some useful tips:[7]

- Students with OCD should remember to be kind to themselves. They have a mental health disorder, hence their ability to think and emotional state may be disordered, through no fault of their own.

- A healthy balance of food, sleep and exercise will help the person to cope with the OCD stress.

- Achievement and success go hand in hand with looking after mental health, so the student needs to find and respect their limits.

- When the intrusion of OCD is extreme, the student shouldn't force themselves into uncomfortable circumstances. As with any illness, there is a limit to how much stress individuals can – and would be expected to – handle. Pre-awareness will help the person with OCD to avoid such situations and thus reduce stress.

- Remember, no two people are the same in the way they handle challenges.

- The support of friends and family can help ease the burden of the secrecy involved with OCD.

- Often, stress is caused by an individual not being able to do what is desired, due to their OCD anxiety. Continuously making excuses is frustrating. Emotional support/expressing their feelings to someone they trust can help reduce the stress. Taking this step isn't always easy, but the OCD-UK website has some helpful advice.

Also, many colleges and universities offer free therapy to students who need it.

Disabled Students' Allowances (DSAs)

Students suffering from OCD may be unaware that they might qualify for extra funding, through Disabled Students' Allowances (DSAs).[8]
(http://www.direct.gov.uk/en/disabledpeople/
educationandtraining/highereducation/dg_10034898)

DSAs provide help for students who, because of their disability, have additional costs. It is available to full- and part-time undergraduate and postgraduate students. Part-time students must be studying for at least 50 per cent of a full-time course. An experienced assessor checks the level of support for which the student is eligible. The person with OCD may need a GP's report to support their claim. DSA money does not count as "income" so the student could still qualify for Income Support or Housing Benefit, should they need to apply.

Further information can be gained from the relevant LEA in England and Wales, or SAAS in Scotland.

....

Interview: Irene Tubbs, therapist

About 40 per cent of my clients are teenagers/young adults. They range from those with borderline OCD to those who have an acute form of it. All of them were born in Britain, but many are of mixed race, such as Asian/White.

My practice treating OCD began twenty years ago, when teenaged clients presented who had anxiety and fear of failure, due to exam pressure. Clients now usually arrive by referral from a parent who has told another parent about my therapy. It is made clear to them that they must ensure the young person wants to come for help, otherwise the treatment won't work. In my experience, OCD is always linked to low self-esteem – also, erratic mood swings; fear of failure; perfectionist traits; fear of being perceived as not good enough by others; relationship difficulties and the natural difficulty of transferring from childhood to adulthood. OCD is the consequence of many life happenings: sometimes it's a dramatic traumatic event, sometimes it's a build-up of constant fear over a long period of time. Although a condition may appear the same between clients, its physical, emotional, behavioural, mental and social effects will surface in different ways.

I also use my knowledge of working with children (I was a teacher) and my professional skills to create a programme specifically for children. This is called Rational Emotive Cognitive Behavioural Education (RECBE) and uses a range of evidence-based tools to "normalize" the obsessive fears of teenagers and children. It then demonstrates constructive self-empowering thinking using behavioural, stress-reducing and relaxation-inducing techniques. These are life skills when they learn them. My personal aim is to get schools to take on board the RECBE programme.

Sometimes with children and teenagers you have the parent to contend with, who is very scared that the person with OCD may harm themselves. They read such frightening stories on the Internet that this belief becomes entrenched. The parents may also become irrational – expecting an instant change or a magic pill to switch their child back to the person they were before. I have never had a teenager not be happy with the therapy – quite the opposite. I offer parents the chance of a few sessions, to understand the consequences of anxiety for themselves and their child. I also offer effective parenting ways to support the child while learning to deal with OCD. These can be very successful, but sometimes even these are not enough, especially if the parent *thinks the therapist is being too effective. The parent may become overly anxious and decide the child should leave therapy and seek psychiatric help, which just reinforces abnormality. This might be because the parent thinks I'm taking over their role, which makes them consider they're not being a good enough parent, which leads to feelings of guilt.*

More parental awareness of the early signs of OCD would be beneficial. My aim is to engage teachers and parents in becoming the normalizing-information person as a child grows up. Then the adults are prepared when the child's OCD behaviour goes outside the realms of normal effective thinking/behaviour/ emotional/physical domains. It's very important that relatives and others close to the OCD sufferer normalize fears – not dismiss them. They have to guard against becoming the young person's "safety net", as this inhibits the child from facing their own fears. If a child wishes me to, I will speak at a school. I rarely advise this. There is a danger of this becoming a safety net for the child too, so as not to face their fears. OCD sufferers can officially disable themselves. Children want this label so that they have a reason to be excused certain things, then it becomes a habit.

Society does not understand OCD well enough at present. There is too long a wait for people to be able to access professional treatment for OCD – especially for children, who are already obsessed by the time they see a doctor. They are very good at hiding it at first. It's also harder for clients generally to alter long-standing patterns of OCD-related behaviour: things will happen in life which will re-trigger their susceptibility towards OCD practices. The more entrenched they are, the more likely they are to resurface.

All OCD rituals are treatable. When people carry out washing/cleansing rituals, it's about: "If I'm cleaner, then I'm a better person." It depends on the irrational belief of the person and how much safety support they get from others as to how long it takes for them to recover. Initially all my clients obsessively worry about issues rather than perform rituals. Of course such disordered thinking eventually triggers rituals, as these initially act as a distraction from the thought.

Families of OCD sufferers are very supportive, in my experience, but they also become very agitated after a while, as their logical responses appear to be ignored by the person with OCD. Carers need a couple of sessions to understand their role in maintaining a child's habits – also, to learn effective ways to stop protecting their offspring. Other children are often very supportive of someone with OCD problems.

Independent Adults with OCD: Advice to Parents, Friends and Partners

USEFUL TIPS

From carers and therapists

- *People in close contact with OCD sufferers should get professional help as soon as possible. Many cases of OCD have already been successfully treated with psychotherapy, though. Having said that, public access to professional treatment for OCD is improving but still has some way to go.*
Rosie Thwaite

- *Make sure the therapist knows properly about OCD.*
James Donald

- *When a person loves someone who is dealing with 10 on the Richter Scale of OCD, they also need to find a way to care for themselves. The whirlwind of rules, structures, emotions*

and pain that the disorder can create is something that can consume all those involved.
Megan Karnes

- *People in close contact with an OCD sufferer can help them by being supportive but not offering too much reassurance. Otherwise, reassurance becomes another aspect of the OCD issue.*
Anna Probert

- *Carers need to be able to be encouraging and patient, especially when there are setbacks.*
Steph Evans

- *John's OCD is noticeably better now he's eating very healthily and taking his medication regularly.*
Helen Greene

- *CBT is an effective treatment for not very acute cases of OCD – when performing obsessions hasn't become a strong habit. It would depend on the case whether it's better to use CBT in conjunction with medication. Gradual exposure to fears, if well tolerated, can be helpful too.*
Ali Knight

- *Treatments which I would definitely advocate are psychodynamic therapy to work with feelings and underlying causes. Also relaxation and gradual exposure techniques, if a client can take it.*
Rosie Thwaite

- *A few sessions of therapy weren't enough.*
Malcolm Riddell

- *Valuable work is being done by UK charities, such as OCD Action and OCD-UK, as well as mental health publishers like Chipmunka.*
Helen Greene

- *Try to accept that this has happened, so you can support the relative or friend. Also, find a good therapist.*
  Michael Jones

- *There's nothing like having a good laugh to help things along. And exercise. I try to get out for a walk every day. I've noticed Ian deals with things better too, if he exercises.*
  Claire Hughes

- *I like going to OCD carers' group meetings.*
  Claire Hughes

- If you are close to someone with OCD, support them and encourage them to get help.
  Anon.

- *My religion and going to church helps me cope.*
  Joyce Winn

- *Try not to lose your patience with the person suffering from OCD.*
  Michael Jones

- *I attend an OCD carers' group – it's turned out to be the best thing I've ever done. It's probably saved our marriage. The group gets on well, no subjects barred. Actually, we spend a lot of the sessions laughing – very cathartic.*
  Kate Shaw

- *Talk to the person with OCD. Encourage them to see a professional who can teach them self-help skills. You should get them some help ASAP.*
  Damien Foster

Sometimes the OCD sufferer will refuse to admit there's a problem, let alone visit a doctor about it. If this happens, you could try offering them educational material about the illness, or leaving it around the house in the hope that they read it. If the person with OCD understands that other people have similar experiences, it will help to ease their feelings of isolation, shame and embarrassment.[1]

This kind of attitude does not help:

> *Both our son and my mother-in-law get impatient*
> *with my husband. I don't think they really*
> *understand the illness or, if they do and feel sorry for*
> *Luke, they don't know how to cope with it except by*
> *trying to chivvy him along.*
> **Heather Smythe**

....

Interview: Ruth

I wish someone had told us to get help for my son Jake sooner, but I probably wouldn't have been able to in the early days as he refused to accept he had a problem. Jake's OCD started around the time his younger brother, Michael, suffered a massive brain injury. Mike was sixteen. Ever since then he's been in a persistent vegetative state.

My relationship with Jake has altered since the OCD began. It's become more of a parent and child relationship, at a time when it would normally be an adult-to-adult one. He's very dependent on me. When things get really bad he resorts to going to bed. Now I understand the illness better, I've learned to separate it from this son I love. But I still need breaks away from Jake for at least an hour a day.

We live in a house surrounded by beautiful countryside, but he rarely goes outside. It's a pity, as exercise really helps him, when I can get him to leave the house. For me, walking my dog is the highlight of my day. For just over nine years, since he was nineteen, Jake's been incapacitated by OCD. It manifests itself in a merciless round of checking locks, windows, taps and electrical sockets. My son lives in constant dread of accidents, burglary or fire. He's also fearful of germs and contamination – he's constantly washing his hands. He can't complete the simplest tasks without reassurance. I guessed he had OCD when he kept checking that the iron was off, and washing too much. The GP confirmed it. Jake obsessively worries about other issues too – OCD has taken over all parts of his life. His stepdad has adjusted and is very kind to him. I would be lost without him.

When the OCD first started, I used to get very impatient. As soon as I suspected he had it, I researched OCD on the Internet. I still read OCD forums online and visit various websites. The doctor has been very helpful; so has an OCD support group I belong to. Unfortunately, it is a round trip of seventy miles to attend; there are no such groups local to us. Going there, though, has been a really valuable experience: it's enabled both Jake and me to meet other sufferers. Before that we felt very isolated.

Holidays are only possible nowadays if we take Jake with us. I have less time to spend with other family members and old friends. My son's mood level is often very low, so I don't feel able to leave him for long. Many of them don't understand OCD anyway, so my relationship with a lot of people I used to be friendly with has changed. My son is now a hoarder too. His bedroom is extremely messy, but he won't allow me or his stepfather in to tidy up. Jake's been unemployed for almost two years, so he's at home a lot. He was bullied at work and, as a result, resigned from his job. He's turned to eating for comfort, so is now quite overweight. I've tried but cannot persuade him to eat healthily. I can't really talk – my eating patterns are all over the place. Sometimes I find it hard to eat anything; other times I overeat.

Jake is on medication. He's been prescribed citalopram, mirtazapime and clorimipramine [brand name Anafranil]. It's hard to say what works and what doesn't, as they keep changing his medicine to see which works best. Jake tried Cognitive Behavioural Therapy but it didn't work for him.

MISDIAGNOSIS

There is an increased recognition of the high number of people with OCD, and the introduction of effective remedies – although as yet no cure. However, in many cases people with the illness continue to remain underdiagnosed and inappropriately treated,[2] as the following case shows.

> ... *Information was really lacking back when James was first diagnosed. People didn't know what they were talking about. Mum took my brother to the doctor, who called in social workers. They hadn't got a clue and wondered if he had Asperger's; then they thought he was schizophrenic. This went on for years until James was nineteen. It was really obvious that he didn't have those conditions, but it was an awful time. My dad doesn't understand James's condition and pretends the OCD isn't there: we don't see him very often.*
>
> *There has been better information about OCD over the past five years. James heard about CBT then, finally, but it didn't really help him – only because it made him think about the illness more, which increased the frequency of the rituals. It took my brother a long time to trust anyone enough to embark on a course of treatment.*

....

Interview: Claire

It still eats away at me wondering why, when my son was first diagnosed, we weren't referred to a more specific treatment place such as the Maudsley [London].

When did you first become aware of Ian's OCD?

When my son was about twenty-two. But of course it must have been longer. Derek and I did not realize anything was wrong, because the doctor we had then referred Ian to a child behaviour therapist. They had a suspicion that things weren't right; they didn't confirm it, though. It wasn't until five years after this that Ian was diagnosed by a psychiatrist. I wish we'd had more help. If only we'd been given the information and support that's available now... Ever since he became ill, Ian has been obsessed with things being "contaminated". It got too much. He never relaxed, and it's hard to see your child so mentally tormented. He's still not coping very well. He can't really manage when the OCD is severe. Ian doesn't like anybody to touch his things without permission. I try to help him by carrying on life as normal and being patient. I worry about his future: I'm in my seventies now.

Do you know if anything in particular caused Ian to become ill?

Possibly it could have been bullying; there was a situation which was badly dealt with. But what's done is done. Ian is on Seroxat now: Prozac didn't work. CBT helped him for a while, but he seems to have slipped back.

....

Interview: Tabitha, a twin

Studies of twins[3] have shown that genes play a larger role when OCD starts in childhood, compared to adulthood.

James is my twin brother. We are twenty-eight. My mum didn't understand his OCD, but she's got better. She's seen documentaries about genetics, though, and blames herself for James's OCD. She feels guilty. So do I. I always felt guilty and would sometimes wonder when we were children why I hadn't got it. Having said that, I do enjoy cleaning... I also find it hard to switch off generally – I'm very proactive.

James lives with his girlfriend now, Louisa; she is coping pretty well. She's very understanding and James is better since they got together. He's thinking of having children with her, so he's been doing a lot of research into genetics and OCD. Apparently the gene is carried on the female chromosome, but usually shows in males. James has said he'll adopt or they will have a surrogate baby (with Louisa giving birth) if there is any chance that their child is going to have OCD. I don't think it would stop me if I decided to have a baby, but I'm not feeling maternal or broody. I'll think about it more if it comes up later.

Mum's having a rest now that James has finally moved out. It was tiring sharing with him, as he made a lot of noise. James's illness used to really upset me, partly because, like Mum, I couldn't sleep. He used to slam doors, but earplugs sorted me out.

When I went to uni, I did a psychology degree. I didn't really recognize it at the time as being due to James's problems. I was just interested in the subject. I'm passionate now about mental illness information being available for everyone. I support MIND and charities like that. I see my brother a few times a year and he has the OCD under control much better now. He was still coughing and making squeaky noises sometimes as part of his rituals last year; now he pulls faces instead. Sometimes he uses his hands strangely and points at things. We are closer now that he manages the OCD better.

....

COPING

Humour can be a helpful coping mechanism for both the sufferer and carer. Many carers have told me that people they know with OCD have a good sense of humour. If you know a person well, carefully judged answers can sometimes lighten situations, as in: "Do you think they will die because of what I just did?" "'Course they will. I've requested invitations to the funeral – it'll be a nice day out."

If someone is coping well in public, but needs time privately to carry out some rituals, finding a loo can help.

> *If we go out to a restaurant, James "binges and purges", as we call it. He saves up his worries. Then, if they get too bad, he goes to the toilet to carry out rituals where no one can see. He can be gone for as long as fifteen minutes.*

WHAT HELP IS AVAILABLE?

It's estimated that around half of GP surgeries in England provide counselling services and support. Access to NHS talking therapy – for example – CBT, will continue to improve over the next few years. Although not everyone with OCD finds counselling and talking therapies helpful, a substantial proportion of sufferers find these services useful.

Support groups

Support groups usually prove very useful. They provide an invaluable space in which carers can share the ups and downs of living with OCD, without feeling disloyal or under pressure. The meetings are often held fortnightly or monthly. The other carers there are dealing with similar issues to you and may be very experienced. They understand what you're going through, trying to help a family member or a friend who has OCD. By their very nature, these groups act as a pooling of knowledge and can be a useful source of information. Other members may be able to provide helpful tips on how to cope.

Seriously consider setting up a local OCD Carers' Support Group yourself. It could be one of the most rewarding things you've ever done. Don't worry about whether you are sufficiently qualified or have enough confidence – you already have the equivalent of a doctorate in OCD by virtue of your experience as a carer.

Feedback from a member of Stevenage OCD Carers' Support Group

> *I've been attending the carers' group for a year on and off; I heard of it through a friend. I come to the meetings because my son suffers from OCD and I hope I can share my experience and help others. We meet every three or four weeks, which is about right for me. I have to travel a long way across Hertfordshire to attend and wouldn't be able to do it more often than that. The group helps me in several ways: it feels supportive and it's an opportunity to share experiences and similar problems. I can listen to other people and, I hope, contribute something helpful.*

A useful listing of nationwide OCD Support Groups, also containing a few OCD Carers' Support Groups, can be found at the back of the *OCD Action Newsletter*.

9

Advice for Young Carers

. . . .

If you are caring for a parent or older relative, do any of these comments sound familiar?[1]

- I'm not exactly allowed out to the shops without Mum.

- She wouldn't let me bring my friends home because she thought we'd make the house dirty.

- I can't move her stuff.

- I do things that hopefully won't affect her, because I don't want to stress her out.

- It was like always treading on eggshells.

- I used to wash my hands a lot, but now I don't do it at all after seeing the state that my mum was in and her panic attacks. I just say, "No, don't do it."

- I know I'll always have the worries, but I'm going to learn ways to handle them, just like my dad does.

- I don't know whether they're real tears or fake.

- It can be very hard sometimes.

OCD in parents or friends can make life difficult. Friendships, leisure, school and family life can all be badly affected. If you are a young person, it might be hard for you to understand the difficulties that adults or friends with OCD are going through. This can result in you – understandably – feeling anxious, confused or frustrated. Young people are now saying that more support and information would help them to cope better with a parent's OCD. Hopefully, this will change things for the better for young carers.

Depending on your age, the burden of dealing with an older relative's OCD may affect you differently. A younger child's leisure time, school and social life will probably be more affected than a teenager's. This is because children can't access these aspects of their lives as easily as teenagers can, without help from adults. For example, travelling to and from friends' houses, and attending clubs.

The person with OCD may constantly seek reassurance or behave oddly, which can be embarrassing. If it's your mother or father, it may seem as if they treat you as though you are the grown-up and they are the child. They may not always seem to be concentrating on what is being said or happening at the time. Perhaps it takes your parent(s) or guardian a long time to carry out a simple task.

The good news is that despite it being hard to live alongside OCD, young people can still often function well. You may have friends and interests, be doing well at school and have clear aspirations. Perhaps you feel proud of the person you know with OCD because they are making progress, and you are pleased that you maintain a good relationship with them.

LOOKING AFTER YOURSELF

It is important that you look after yourself as well as possible.

Seek help; don't suffer in silence caring for an older person with OCD. Go to the GP or a counsellor, or another adult you trust, and tell them what's happening. Ask for counselling if you feel you need it, to help you cope at home. You are not being disloyal by doing this. If the GP doesn't know much about OCD, there are "icebreaker" questions on the OCD-UK website – http://www.ocduk.org/ice-breaker – which can be printed off. If you don't have access to a computer/printer, the questions can be requested by post from the charity. You will need to enclose a stamped addressed envelope.

Obviously be careful if you surf the Internet for OCD information: there is a lot of inaccurate and possibly frightening material out there. There are some useful websites listed at the end of this book.

Try to eat healthily, take exercise and get enough sleep. It does help when coping with stress. Granted, sleeping might be difficult if the person with OCD makes a lot of noise at night. Earplugs can be a cheap solution, though.

A few mothers with OCD have been found to be manipulative, using guilt, or being overprotective and restrictive, to try to control their children. This is because they are trying to stop events occurring which frighten them. If this is happening to you, it might be that they are frightened of harm coming to you when you go out.

A parent with OCD can sometimes be very strict and critical towards their children if they show signs of having OCD too.

WHAT TO DO TO HELP

It is important not to give in to OCD. If the person with OCD asks you to do something for them – for example, check the front door is locked – refuse to do so. This is difficult to do, as you will probably want to help them, and you may feel sorry for them. But colluding with their rituals helps the inner OCD bully become stronger. You should try to keep calm, and be pleasant and patient, showing the person you care about them, but that you're acting from a position of goodwill. Try not to give in to emotional manipulation or repeated requests for reassurance. The friend or relative has OCD; it's not their fault. You can reassure them once, if really necessary, but after that refuse to be drawn into agreement.

The thoughts of the person with OCD are intrusive, and nag the person into carrying out certain behaviour, such as tapping something five times. This offers them a soothing promise that such an action will stop them worrying or feeling fear about something else. Of course, this is wrong. The person might feel better for a millisecond after tapping something five times, but soon the OCD will force them to carry out the behaviour twice as often, so they'll quickly be tapping something ten times, and so on, so, if your mother asks you to check the stove is off when you know she's already done it, say no. That way, the OCD doesn't win.

As a therapist has said:

> *The person you love may get increasingly upset and even emotionally aggressive. "OK," you say. "I give in, just this time." You have quiet; they seem better – and you've both just done the opposite of what would help either of you.*

It would be helpful if you were to try to encourage the person with OCD to seek outside help. There is no shame in this: many people suffer from the condition. It does not mean they are mad. Parents with OCD are worried about the impact it has on their children, even if they don't tell them. They are sometimes frightened to raise their anxieties with mental health services, though, in case they are judged or found to be bad parents. If your parent hasn't sought professional help for their OCD yet, try to persuade them to go to their GP.

Treatment may be recommended by the doctor. Increasingly, there is free counselling and therapy available. This is due to the Improving Access to Psychological Therapies (IAPT) programme. Also, you could encourage the person with OCD to attend a support group.

This is an excerpt from an interview with Tabitha, the twin sister of a young man with OCD, but it may be something you've experienced with someone older:

> *I never knew if what I said would set off his OCD.*
> *It was like walking on eggshells. It got worse if James*
> *was tired. There used to be words he couldn't bear to*
> *listen to – they would trigger the OCD – like "devil"*
> *or "loser". He still can't bear people not making the*
> *best of themselves. He calls them "scumbags".*

Employment and
the Workplace

> *My brother is happy at work now, and the people
> in the office are fine with him. He's a civil engineer.
> There was a bit of trouble at work when James was
> younger: he used to try to hide the OCD, but it
> made for stress and aggression.*
> **Tabitha**

EMPLOYERS – UK

If you are an employer with an average-sized company, the
chances are that one of your employees has OCD. This does
not mean they can't do their job well – in fact the person could
easily be an efficient workaholic. However, employees with
OCD may work more slowly than others, due to obsessive
checking or perfectionism.

Individuals with OCD are often highly driven but, somewhat
surprisingly, may believe they are inept and helpless. Their
self-perception of helplessness is linked to a fear of being
overwhelmed and unable to function.

Someone with OCD will probably think:[1]

- If I or others don't perform at the highest standards, we will fail.

- I know what's best; you have to do it my way.

- If I fail in this, I am a failure as a person.

- I must be in control.

- I must do everything virtually just right.

- Why do I always slip up?

In such circumstances, the individual with OCD may end up slave-driving themselves or others. Due to their perfectionist standards, people with OCD are also prone to experiencing regret, disappointment, anger or anxiety – towards both themselves and others. Unless colleagues are aware and make allowances for the condition, it may lead to stress in the workplace, even though most sufferers are skilled at concealing their OCD for fear of ridicule or incomprehension. When serious failure occurs, though, they may become depressed.

Benefits of working with employees with OCD and similar conditions

Considerable benefits can accrue if employers and employees work in partnership. It also reflects well on the employer and the company itself if they employ people with conditions such as OCD.

Many employees with OCD feel they can't talk to their employers or line managers, due to the stigma still sometimes attached to mental illness. There is also a fear of being stereotyped and bullied. If this happens, it naturally leads to higher absence and lower productivity by staff members.

You can improve business performance in your organization in the following ways:

- Sickness levels can be managed by providing a better workplace atmosphere.

- Give your employees the opportunity to discuss matters regarding their performance.

- Consider providing training for managers to help them to understand OCD, or direct them to www.OCDtodayuk. org, where members of staff are happy to provide information.

Equality Act 2010

The duty for employers to make reasonable adjustments at work for people with mental or physical disabilities is governed by the Equality Act 2010. This replaces the Disability Discrimination Act 1995.

It imposes a duty on the employer to take steps to prevent the disabled person from being placed at a disadvantage compared to other staff. However, not all people suffering from OCD will need adjustments in order to successfully perform their jobs.

Common sense is the key. If you have an employee with OCD who is experiencing difficulties, you could offer them an existing vacancy within the company in which they would feel more comfortable. Are they finding it difficult handling money as a cashier? Offer them a back-office position. Should the individual have problems with punctuality, perhaps this could be accommodated by allowing them to arrive at work later and leave later. It's also a good move to inform an employee with OCD of any adjustments at work as soon as possible, as they need reassurance more than most about changes.

Useful websites
http://ocdtodayuk.org/ocd_information/employers.html
http://www.ocdaction.org.uk/files/2010/04/Employing-People-with-OCD-web.pdf

Helping someone with OCD to find a job in the UK

Present UK government policy is to enable those with mental health problems to return to work. There are now several groups which provide support for people with OCD who wish to become an employee, or to return to work.

The local Job Centre should have access to a Disability Employment Adviser. If they don't, the person with OCD should ask to speak to a Personal Adviser or New Deal Job Broker.

They can also find out about specialist schemes in their area by asking their local CAB, social services, or Community Mental Health Team.

TO DECLARE OR NOT TO DECLARE

Many people with OCD are worried about being discriminated against if they declare their condition on job application forms. This area of employment law is constantly developing, so if the applicant is still in a dilemma about disclosing their OCD after seeking general guidance, they could seek legal advice. Free legal advice is available from the Community Legal Service Helpline. Guidance can also be obtained from organizations such as:

• the Disability Law Service

• the Equality and Human Rights Commission

• ACAS

• the TUC – which provides a number of useful booklets for both employers and employees

• the Mind legal helpline.

It is now unlawful for an employer to ask a job applicant about their health before offering work – this includes conditional offers of work.

For job seekers with OCD, two pieces of legislation could influence whether or not they disclose their OCD to the employer. The Equality Act 2010 provides a streamlined law to tackle discrimination more effectively. If the applicant has OCD, this Act may protect their rights in terms of accessing treatment, employment, goods and services and housing. Public Sector Equality Duty is part of the Act and came into force in the UK in 2011, replacing the Disability Equality Duty. This covers all the protected areas: age, disability, gender, gender reassignment, pregnancy and maternity, race, religion and belief, and sexual orientation. The Equality Act 2010 states that employers are not allowed to discriminate against disabled people. OCD can be classed as a disability (at the point of diagnosis) under the Act.

Decisions about disclosure of health problems are deeply personal, of course, but bodies such as the TUC encourage members to disclose mental health problems to employers. The onus is then on the employer to make reasonable adjustments. It can be very stressful, too, for people with OCD to feel they have to hide the illness. If the person with OCD decides to disclose any mental health conditions, they have the right for such information to remain confidential under the Data Protection Act 1998.

It's worth remembering that if the potential employer has made reasonable attempts to find out about an OCD sufferer's health condition and they haven't disclosed it, they may not be able to make a claim for discrimination under the Equality Act 2010. The employer can argue that they were unaware of the employee's condition. The Health and Safety at Work etc. Act 1974 states that if an employee's disability could cause implications for their health and safety, or that of their colleagues, they must tell their employer.

If you are a person with OCD, check if the potential or current employer has clear equity policies in place. A proactive employer will often have such policies already set up. Check the documentation available within the organization, perhaps with Human Resources, to see the type of protection available for employees with OCD.

Employers may be happy to increase intake of employees with disabilities; it reflects well on their organization. A worker with OCD is likely to feel empowered if they are offered a job knowing that their employer is aware of their condition and willing to make adjustments (if necessary) to aid them.

EMPLOYERS – AUSTRALIA

OCD is not uncommon, with around three in every 100 people developing the condition at some time in their lives – more than 450,000 Australians.

As it says correctly at http://jobaccess.gov.au/Employers/Pages/home.aspx:

> *Like all employees, people with disability bring a range of skills, talents and abilities to the workplace. They work in all sorts of jobs with many holding tertiary and trade qualifications. Many businesses already employ people with disability because it makes good business sense.*
>
> *Employees with disability are:*
>
> - **Reliable** – *people with disability take fewer days off, take less sick leave and stay in jobs longer than other workers*
>
> - **Productive** – *once in the right job, people with disability perform as well as other employees*
>
> - **Affordable** – *recruitment, insurance cover and compensation costs are lower. People with disability have fewer compensation incidents and accidents at work in comparison to other employees, and*

- **Good for business** – *people with disability build strong connections with customers. They boost staff morale and loyalty by helping to create a diverse workforce. Teamwork is enhanced. Real cost savings are realised through less turnover, recruitment and retraining costs.*

  Hiring people with disability adds to the organisation's overall diversity. It builds the company's image among its staff, community and customers with positive benefits to the employer label.

If it turns out to be necessary, there are ways that people with OCD can be helped in the workplace so that they can better manage their symptoms and continue to work. These include:

- the employee seeking professional help

- the provision of training for other staff members, so that they are aware of mental health issues, especially for staff that may never have come into contact with mental health illnesses

- providing a support therapist for the person

- reducing incidence of anything that may trigger the person's OCD; for example, if it is triggered by being in a dirty environment, the employer could make sure they are assigned to a cleaner environment.

SANE has been working with Australian businesses for over twenty years. SANE has a Mindful Employer programme and provides advice, information and referrals on mental illness.

Useful websites
http://www.mindfulemployer.org/
http://www.mindfulemployer.org/sane

EMPLOYERS – USA

Once an employee discloses having OCD, the Americans with Disabilities Act (ADA) protects the employee from being discriminated against due to mental illness. ADA law requires employers to provide reasonable accommodation at the employee's request. Reasonable accommodation for an employee with OCD may include:

- **Eliminating minor job duties that challenge the employee's condition**
  If your employee compulsively checks things, reassign tasks requiring counting or verification, or get a job coach to help the employee focus on the bigger picture.

- **Offering flexible schedules**
  Allow an employee with OCD to make up hours missed because of doctor's appointments. If your employee's medication causes drowsiness in the morning, allow the employee to come in later and work later.

- **Considering structural needs**
  An employee obsessed with having things "just so" may appreciate having an assigned parking place.

- **Making job performance expectations clear**
  Help the employee set professional goals. Encourage them to continue with medication and treatment.

Useful websites
https://www.achievesolutions.net/achievesolutions/en/covacare/Content.do?contentId=3961
http://www.ocfoundation.org/EO_Americans_with_Disabilities_Act.aspx

A friend's experience

I feel that there has been some discrimination towards Isabella at work. When she was having her group therapy, there was a whole debate about whether she needed to make up the time she was out of the office; whether she should take it as annual leave, or be allowed it as medical treatment. I am sure if someone were having treatment for a debilitating physical condition, no such debate would take place. I doubt, for example, that someone having chemotherapy or physiotherapy would be expected to make the time up, or take it as leave.

I am unsure how this was resolved, but it left me with the distinct impression that there is a lack of understanding in our workplace of the impact of mental health issues. My friend is allowed to start work later than her colleagues (9:30 a.m.), because of her difficulties in getting out of the house in the morning. However, I don't think her employers understand that without continuing efforts and/or treatment, there is a risk of her getting worse and not making it into work at all.

Isabella has spoken to me once of her feeling that she might as well give up and stay at home, but I've encouraged her to persevere. My fear is that she would rapidly slide backwards with more time on her hands to focus on her OCD activities.

"OCD shouldn't be a barrier to productive work…" say Donna Gillet and Michael McKee, in "Strategies for Coping with OCD in the Workplace".[2] In their experience, both clients and staff realize the value of employment as therapy. The immediate benefits for self-esteem are clear, while the demands and structure of work challenge the person with OCD to function in spite of their disorder.

It could help the entire household if you can aid someone with OCD in finding employment. OCD sufferers – like most people – often feel pride and relief in having a job and earning power. Employment can also reduce OCD symptoms. Pre-employment concerns to be addressed might include a reduction of morning rituals such as hand-washing and door- or oven-checking. A plan for transportation to work must be made in advance. This minimizes the potential for compulsions. (Particularly true for those with obsessive fears of injuring others in driving accidents.)

It is recommended that a nervous client with OCD who would like to return to work should first seek a volunteer job. By this means, important elements of the employment process could be practised before the client went ahead with the more anxiety-provoking test of gaining a paying job.

Endpaper

. . . .

Experiencing OCD is a living hell. I've met hundreds of people with OCD and talked to thousands, as the people around them are also affected. What I would say to those who have not had the good fortune to know someone with OCD, is that people who experience this disorder are thoughtful, sensitive and too good! I feel fortunate to have known so many – I mean that. Don't forget the person who has OCD: they need you.
Megan Karnes, therapist

Appendix A:
OCD and the Brain

There are contradictory views as to whether the brains of people with OCD differ from other people's. Apparently brain-imaging studies[1] have shown abnormalities in several parts of the brains of people with OCD. These include the thalamus, caudate nucleus, orbital cortex and cingulate gyrus. Abramowitz,[2] though, dismisses the idea of some gross abnormality being responsible for producing the illogical symptoms of OCD. To date there is little compelling evidence that these symptoms are caused by abnormal brain structure or function.

The orbital cortex is in the front part of the brain, above the eyes. It informs us when something is wrong, or we should avoid something. A study compared the brains of people with OCD to those of people without it. MRIs show a larger cortex (Jenike, Breiter *et al.*, 1996). It's like an early warning system in the brain, and seems to work overtime in people with OCD.

The caudate nucleus[3] is situated deep in the brain centre and controls the filtering of thoughts. Normally, unnecessary information is ignored. People with OCD, though, are overwhelmed by intrusive thoughts and urges which the caudate nucleus doesn't sift out. The caudate of an OCD sufferer behaves like the doorman of an

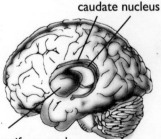

caudate nucleus

lentiform nucleus
(putamen and globus pallidus)

apartment building, who does a poor job keeping out burglars.[4]
So, to summarize:

- The thalamus sends messages from other parts of the body, making an OCD sufferer hyper-aware of everything that's happening.

- The caudate nucleus opens the gate and allows in unwanted intrusive thoughts.

- The orbital cortex mixes thoughts with emotions, then shouts, "Something's wrong here – take cover!"

- The cingulate gyrus orders the person with OCD to carry out compulsions, to relieve the anxiety the rest of their brain has heaped on them.

- While all this is going on, their synaptic clefts are screaming: "Send in more serotonin. We're running low!"

NEUROSURGERY

Cingulotomy is the most common neurosurgical procedure for OCD.[5] Other surgical operations include anterior capsulotomy, subcaudate tractotomy and limbic leukotomy.

Appendix B:
Genetics

It's natural for parents to wonder how much OCD is an inherited condition if they see it manifested in their child, and a family member also has the illness.

Fineberg[1] says that OCD is considered to be one of the most strongly inherited mental disorders. Approximately one-fifth of nuclear family members of OCD sufferers show signs of OCD, and the younger the person, the more likely they are to have a first-degree relative with it. Geller suggested in 1998 that those with child-onset OCD may be more likely to have a blood relative with the condition. Other studies indicate that there may be a higher rate of OCD, subclinical OCD, tics and Tourette's syndrome among relatives of people with OCD (Alsobrook and Pauls, 1998).OCD research done since 1930 has shown OCD traits in blood relatives of 20 to 40 per cent of studied cases (Yaryura-Tobias and Neziroglu, 1997b).[2]

Most children experience some obsessional symptoms, but in only a minority do these symptoms develop into OCD.[3] If they do, it's been suggested that the average age of OCD onset is at around twenty years old, with the illness peaking in early teens and again in the early twenties. In 80 per cent of cases, symptoms present before the person is eighteen. Males develop OCD earlier than females, at around nine years old. Girls usually develop OCD around the age of puberty.

Appendix C:
Parents and Their Children

Adults with OCD fear that they might be judged, found to be bad parents or, at worst, that their children will be removed from their care.[1]

It's been suggested that dependent children should receive an assessment, where they are at risk as a result of parental OCD (NICE, 2005). Collaboration between adult and children's services to safeguard the children of parents with mental health problems was put into policy by the Department of Health in 2006.

Black *et al.* in 2003 studied seven- to eighteen-year-olds with parents who had OCD. They found these children to be at greater risk of anxiety, depression, social problems, and lifetime OCD. This study has since been criticized as being unnecessarily pessimistic.

Weinberg and Tronick in 1998 studied infants of parents with OCD, depression, or panic disorder. They discovered that mother–infant interactions and the infants' social and emotional functioning were compromised in all groups.

In 2009, Challacombe and Salkovskis also identified difficulties in mother–child interactions. They compared mothers with OCD panic disorder, and healthy controls, with seven- to fourteen-year-olds.Mothers with OCD were more critical and emotionally over-involved; they also felt they would be more punitive if their child behaved obsessively.

Interviews were conducted with ten thirteen- to nineteen-year-olds, including siblings. It was found that parental OCD presented challenges and placed a burden on the children, for which they didn't receive adequate support. The issues raised by parental OCD seemed similar to other parental mental health problems, but the results suggested that the child's developmental stage may be a significant influence.

In an unpublished dissertation (Belman, 1999) five daughters aged fifteen to twenty-five were interviewed regarding their mother's OCD. The results suggested mothers used guilt, manipulation, overprotection and restriction to avoid feared situations. The daughters took on parental roles and experienced frustration and anxiety.

Several authors have called for more in-depth exploration of the experiences of offspring of parents with mental health problems.[2] This research could also inform clinical practice, to help prevent problems that might lie ahead for these children.

Appendix D:
Counselling and Psychotherapy

During research for this book, I emailed and/or phoned approximately 100 therapists, male and female. They were almost all members of either the British Association for Behavioural and Cognitive Psychotherapies (BABCP), or the British Association for Counselling & Psychotherapy (BACP). This threw up some interesting responses. The majority of mental health professionals I contacted were pleasant and professional, but many others didn't respond at all. There was the surprisingly arrogant phone manner of a few therapists to contend with, plus the unreliable behaviour of several more. The latter practitioners initially sounded very enthusiastic about meeting up, or completing a questionnaire, but I didn't hear from them again. (I contacted them once more to check, but still nothing.)

I was concerned by responses from eight other professionals on these websites, who professed to treat people with OCD in their advertising, but did not feel sufficiently *au fait* with the condition to be cited. This naturally does not apply to anyone quoted in this book.

Analysts have actually known for many years that their form of therapy – analysis – is of no value to people with OCD.[1] In 1965 – just prior to the initiation of programmes of research using behaviour therapy for OCD – the *British Journal of Psychiatry* declared: "Traditional efforts to treat OCD are a complete failure and should you encounter a patient with this condition, tell them gently that nothing can be done." Since there have been no appreciable advances in psychoanalytic theory for OCD since then, the same statement still holds true.[2]

Bibliography

Abramowitz, Jonathan S., *Understanding and Treating Obsessive–Compulsive Disorder: A Cognitive-Behavioral Approach*, London: Routledge, 2005.

Anthony, Martin M., Christine Purdon, Laura J. Summerfeldt, eds, *Psychological Treatment of Obsessive–Compulsive Disorder: Fundamentals and Beyond*, Washington DC: American Psychological Association, 2007.

Arnold, Lesley M., "A Case Series of Women with Postpartum-Onset Obsessive–Compulsive Disorder", *Primary Care Companion J. Clin. Psychiatry*, August 1999.

Beck, Aaron T., Arthur Freeman, Denise D. Davis, *Cognitive Therapy of Personality Disorders*, New York, NY: Guilford Press, 2006.

De Silva, Padmal, Stanley Rachman, *Obsessive-Compulsive Disorder, The Facts*, Oxford: Oxford University Press, 2004.

Fineberg, Naomi, Donatella Marazziti, Dan J. Stein, *Obsessive Compulsive Disorder: A Practical Guide*, London: Martin Dunitz, 2001.

Griffiths, Jennifer, Emma Norris, Paul Stallard, Shane Matthews (2011 online), "Living with parents with obsessive–compulsive disorder: children's lives and experiences", *Psychology and Psychotherapy: Theory, Research and Practice*, Vol. 85, Issue 1, 2012.

Hyman, Bruce M., Cherry Pedrick, *The OCD Workbook: Your Guide to Breaking Free from Obsessive Compulsive Disorder*, Oakland, CA: New Harbinger Publications Inc., 1999.

Leahy, Robert L., Stephen J. F. Holland, Lata K. McGinn, *Treatment Plans and Interventions for Depression and Anxiety Disorders*, New York, NY: Guilford Press, 2011.

Menzies, Ross G., Padmal de Silva, eds, "Repetitive and Iterative Thinking in Psychopathology", Theoretical Accounts of OCD, *Obsessive Compulsive Disorder: Theory, Research and Treatment*, NJ: Wiley, 2003.

Wilhelm, Sabine, Gail S. Steketee, *Cognitive Therapy for Obsessive–Compulsive Disorder: A Guide for Professionals* CA: New Harbinger Publications Inc., 2006.

OTHER SOURCES

International OCD Foundation, Inc., Boston, MA 02109.

WEB

http://en.wikipedia.org/wiki/Obsessive%E2%80%93compulsive_disorder

http://www.anxietyuk.org.uk/about-anxiety/anxiety-disorders/obsessive-compulsive-disorder-ocd/

http://www.ncbi.nlm.nih.gov/pubmedhealth/PMH0001926/

http://www.nhs.uk/conditions/Obsessive-compulsive-disorder/Pages/Introduction.aspx

http://www.ocdaction.org.uk/support-info/

http://www.ocduk.org/

http://www.ocfoundation.org/whatisocd.aspx?gclid=CPaTspq3pqoCFYMK fAod2G2qXA

OCD-UK website, 3/8/2011

http://ocdtodayuk.org/

http://www.michaelmckeephd.com/workplace_ocd.htm

http://www.babcp.com

http://ocd.about.com/od/typesofocd/a/postpartum_OCD.htm

http://www.pregnancy-info.net/postpartum_obsessive_compulsive_disorder. html

http://www.washingtonpost.com/wp-dyn/content/article/2006/03/06/ AR2006030601145_2.html?sub=new

http://www.ocfoundation.org/hoarding/hoarding. aspx?id=687&terms=hoarding

http://www.compulsive-hoarding.org/OCD.html

http://www.studenthealth.co.uk/advice/advice.asp?adviceID=220

http://edition.cnn.com/2010/HEALTH/expert.q.a/05/04/emdr.therapy. raison/index.html

http://www.mayoclinic.com/health/hoarding/ds00966/dsection=treatments-and-drugs

http://psychcentral.com/lib/2012/ocd-treatment-for-contamination-fears/ all/1/

http://www.nhs.uk/Livewell/counselling/Pages/Accesstotherapy.aspx

A nationwide listing of UK OCD Support Groups, also containing a few OCD Carers' Support Groups, can be found at the back of the *OCD Action Newsletter*.

Useful Websites
and Organizations

As well as the UK OCD information, other European organizations can be found at: http://www.nice.org.uk/nicemedia/pdf/cg031publicinfo.pdf (NICE guidelines).

Child and Adolescent Mental Health
http://www.camh.org.uk/

List of useful (international) websites
http://www.geonius.com/ocd/organizations.html

EABCT
The European Association for Behavioural and Cognitive Therapies brings together forty-four individual associations from thirty-one different countries.
http://www.eabct.com/
http://eabct.glimworm.com/index.jsp?USMID=112

AUSTRALIA
Useful international list of OCD organizations and support groups, etc.
http://www.geonius.com/ocd/organizations.html

ReachOut Australia
http://au.reachout.com/find/articles/obsessive-compulsive-disorder-ocd

Anxiety Recovery Centre, Victoria
http://www.arcvic.org.au/

For employers
http://www.mindfulemployer.org/

Books about anxious children and animals set in Australia (for five- to twelve-year olds)
http://www.worrybusters.com/books.htm

CANADA

Useful international list of OCD organizations and support groups, etc.
http://www.geonius.com/ocd/organizations.html

Anxiety Disorders Clinic, McMaster University Medical Center, HHS, Hamilton, Ontario
http://www.ocdcanada.com/
http://www.macanxiety.com/

Canadian Mental Health Association
http://www.cmha.ca/mental_health/obsessive-compulsive-disorder/

The Canadian OCD Network
http://canadianocdnetwork.com/

How to cope when your child has OCD...
http://www.canadianliving.com/moms/family_life/how_to_cope_when_a_family_member_has_obsessive_compulsive_disorder.php

NEW ZEALAND

Information on OCD
http://www.familydoctor.co.nz/index.asp?U=conditions&A=32756
http://www.everybody.co.nz/page-d042b8ad-e258-4ca3-8ea5-f0296af9701b.aspx

http://www.phobic.org.nz/pdf/obsessive_compulsive_disorder.pdf
http://www.stuff.co.nz/life-style/wellbeing/2001478/
Childhood-beginnings-for-OCD

Anxiety support group with info about OCD, offering support, Canterbury-based
http://anxietysupport.org.nz/about-anxiety/obsessive-compulsive-disorder/

SOUTH AFRICA
The South African Depression and Anxiety Group
http://www.sadag.org/index.php?option=com_content&task=view&id=48&Itemid=74
http://www.sahealthinfo.org/mentalhealth/ocdhelp.htm

Data on OCD in black South Africans appears to be limited at present.

USA
American Psychiatric Association
Phone: (888) 357-7924
Email: apa@psych.org
Website: www.psych.org

American Psychological Association
Phone: (800) 374-2721
Website: www.apa.org

Americans with Disabilities Act
US Department of Justice
Phone: (800) 514-0301
Website: www.ada.gov

Anxiety Disorders Association of America
Phone: (240) 485-1001
Email: information@adaa.org

Website: www.adaa.org

Anxiety Disorders Foundation
Phone: (262) 567-6600
Email: info@anxietydisordersfoundation.org
Website: www.anxietydisordersfoundation.org

Association for Behavioral and Cognitive Therapies
Phone: (212) 647-1890
Website: www.abct.org

Cover the Uninsured
Phone: (877) 655-CTUW
Email: info@covertheuninsured.org
Website: http://covertheuninsured.org

Individuals with Disabilities
Education Act (IDEA)
Phone: (202) 884-8215
Website: http://idea.ed.gov

National Alliance on Mental Illness
Phone: (800) 950-NAMI
Website: http://www.nami.org

National Institute of Mental Health
Phone: (866) 615-6464
Website: www.nimh.nih.gov

National Mental Health Information Center
Phone: (800) 789-2647
Website: http://mentalhealth.samhsa.gov

National Suicide Prevention Lifeline
Phone: (800) 273-8255
Website: www.suicidepreventionlifeline.org

Obsessive Compulsive Anonymous
World Services (OCA)

Phone: (516) 741-4901
Email: west24th@aol.com
Website: www.obsessivecompulsiveanonymous.org

International OCD Foundation (IOCDF)
http://www.ocfoundation.org/

Obsessive Compulsive Information Center (OCIC)
Phone: (608) 827-2470
Email: mim@miminc.org
Website: www.miminc.org/aboutocic.asp

Trichotillomania Learning Center (TLC)
Phone: (831) 457-1004
Email: info@trich.org
Website: http://www.trich.org

Yahoo OCD Support Groups (Online)
Website: health.groups.yahoo.com/group/
OCDSupportGroups/links

Notes

. . . .

Chapter 1

1. Padmal de Silva, Stanley Rachman, *Obsessive Compulsive Disorder, The Facts*, Oxford: Oxford University Press, 2004.
2. Bruce M. Hyman, Cherry Pedrick, *The OCD Workbook: Your Guide to Breaking Free from Obsessive-Compulsive Disorder*, Oakland, CA: New Harbinger Publications Inc., 1999.
3. http://en.wikipedia.org/wiki/Obsessive%E2%80%93compulsive_disorder
(a) Eric Hollander, Dan J. Stein, "Diagnosis and Assessment". *Obsessive–Compulsive Disorders*, Nforma Health Care, 1997, p. 1.
(b) Gary Null, "Obsessive–Compulsive Disorder", Get Healthy Now Seven Stories Press, 2006, p. 269.
(c) Jonathan S. Abramowitz, *Understanding and Treating Obsessive–Compulsive Disorder: A Cognitive-Behavioral Approach*, London: Routledge, 2005.
4. Padmal de Silva, Stanley Rachman, *Obsessive Compulsive Disorder, The Facts*.
5. Bruce M. Hyman, Cherry Pedrick, *The OCD Workbook: Your Guide to Breaking Free from Obsessive Compulsive Disorder*.
6. Padmal de Silva, Stanley Rachman, *Obsessive Compulsive Disorder, The Facts*.
7. Jonathan S. Abramowitz, *Understanding and Treating Obsessive–Compulsive Disorder: A Cognitive-Behavioral Approach*.
8. http://www.pregnancy-info.net/postpartum_obsessive_compulsive_disorder.html

Chapter 3

1. Padmal de Silva, Stanley Rachman, *Obsessive Compulsive Disorder, The Facts*.
2. http://www.ocduk.org/
3. Aaron T. Beck, Arthur Freeman, Denise D. Davis, *Cognitive Therapy of Personality Disorders*, New York, NY: Guilford Press, 2006.

Chapter 4
1. International OCD Foundation Inc., Boston, MA 02109
www.ocfoundation.org
2. http://www.ocfoundation.org/hoarding/hoarding.
aspx?id=687&terms=hoarding
International OCD Foundation Inc., Boston, MA 02109
www.ocfoundation.org
3. Bruce M. Hyman, Cherry Pedrick, *The OCD Workbook: Your Guide to Breaking Free from Obsessive Compulsive Disorder*.
4. *Ibid.*
5. http://www.mayoclinic.com/health/hoarding/ds00966/
dsection=treatments-and-drugs

Chapter 5
1. Bruce M. Hyman, Cherry Pedrick, *The OCD Workbook: Your Guide to Breaking Free from Obsessive Compulsive Disorder*.
2. Bruce M. Hyman, Cherry Pedrick Pedrick, *The OCD Workbook*.
3. International OCD Foundation Inc., Boston, MA 02109
www.ocfoundation.org
4. Bruce M. Hyman, Cherry Pedrick, *The OCD Workbook*.
5. *Ibid.*
6. International OCD Foundation Inc., Boston, MA 02109
www.ocfoundation.org
7. *Ibid.*

Chapter 6
1. Bruce M. Hyman, Cherry Pedrick, *The OCD Workbook: Your Guide to Breaking Free from Obsessive Compulsive Disorder*.
2. http://psychcentral.com/lib/2012/ocd-treatment-for-
contamination-fears/all/1/

Chapter 7
1. Bruce M. Hyman, Cherry Pedrick, *The OCD Workbook: Your Guide to Breaking Free from Obsessive Compulsive Disorder*.
2. *Ibid.*
3. International OCD Foundation Inc., Boston, MA 02109
www.ocfoundation.org
4. *Ibid.*
5. *Ibid.*
6. http://www.ocduk.org/
7. http://www.studenthealth.co.uk/advice/advice.asp?adviceID=220

8. http://www.studenthealth.co.uk/advice/advice asp?adviceID=220
http://www.ocduk.org/

Chapter 8
1. http://www.ocduk.org/
2. Naomi Fineberg, Donatella Marazziti, Dan J. Stein, *Obsessive Compulsive Disorder: A Practical Guide,* London: Martin Dunitz, 2001.
3. Bruce M. Hyman, Cherry Pedrick, *The OCD Workbook: Your Guide to Breaking Free from Obsessive Compulsive Disorder.*

Chapter 9
1. Jennifer Griffiths, Emma Norris, Paul Stallard, Shane Matthews (2011 online)
"Living with parents with obsessive–compulsive disorder: children's lives and experiences", *Psychology and Psychotherapy: Theory, Research and Practice, Vol. 85, Issue 1,* 2012, pp. 68–82.

Chapter 10
1. Aaron T. Beck, Arthur Freeman, Denise D. Davis, *Cognitive Therapy of Personality Disorders.*
2. D. Gillet, M. McKee, "Strategies for Coping with OCD in the Workplace", Obsessive Compulsive Foundation Newsletter, 12 (2), 1998.

Appendix A
1. Bruce M. Hyman, Cherry Pedrick, *The OCD Workbook: Your Guide to Breaking Free from Obsessive Compulsive Disorder.*
2. Jonathan S. Abramowitz, *Understanding and Treating Obsessive–Compulsive Disorder: A Cognitive-Behavioral Approach.*
3. Bruce M. Hyman, Cherry Pedrick, *The OCD Workbook.*
4. *Ibid.*
5. *Ibid.*

Appendix B
1. Bruce M. Hyman, Cherry Pedrick, *The OCD Workbook: Your Guide to Breaking Free from Obsessive Compulsive Disorder.*
2. Naomi Fineberg, Donatella Marazziti, Dan J. Stein, *Obsessive Compulsive Disorder: A Practical Guide.*
3. *Ibid.*

Appendix C
1. Jennifer Griffiths, Emma Norris, Paul Stallard, Shane Matthews (2011 online)
"Living with parents with obsessive–compulsive disorder: children's lives and experiences", *Psychology and Psychotherapy: Theory, Research and Practice*.
6. *Ibid.*

Appendix D
1. http://psychcentral.com/lib/2012/ocd-treatment-for-contamination-fears/all/1/
2. *Ibid.*